BASICS

LOADBEARING
SYSTEMS

\\ ALFRED MEISTERMANN \\

BASICS

LOADBEARING SYSTEMS

BIRKHÄUSER
BASEL · BOSTON · BERLIN

CONTENTS

FOREWORD

When constructing a building, we need to know how its structural properties function. Loadbearing elements can be the dominant features of the design, or simply an invisible substructure – but a building is always based on its loadbearing structure. It holds the building together, distributes loads into the ground, and guarantees stability. An understanding of loadbearing – its structural principles and the specific qualities of individual loadbearing systems – is fundamental to applying these principles sensibly in the design process and developing a solution that suits the materials and the construction method.

It is often difficult, particularly at the beginning of a course when there is so much new material to assimilate, to work one's way into the complexities of statics and loadbearing theory. *Basics Loadbearing Systems* bridges the fields of architecture and civil engineering and explains the fundamentals of loadbearing structure theory simply, comprehensibly and chronologically. To help general understanding, the author first explains the loads and forces occurring in a building using examples and simple contexts. He introduces typical loadbearing structural elements and shows loadbearing systems and structures for the different building types that planners can use for their designs. The compact knowledge conveyed here makes it possible for students to work with loadbearing structures in an integrated way, and thus be able to design creatively.

Bert Bielefeld, Editor

LOADS AND FORCES

LOADBEARING STRUCTURES AND STATICS

A great deal of philosophizing can be done about how design relates to construction. Very different positions can be taken, but they are always two sides of the same coin. Designing spaces means defining them, by applying theory to structures that will need to be realized. Knowing about structures is therefore one of the fundamentals of architectural theory. It is very rare for the architect him- or herself to vouch for the stability of constructions. But he or she should be in a position to select structural elements correctly at the early design stages and to assess the dimensions needed for them realistically. The next step is usually to develop the loadbearing system with a structural engineer. To be able to work together effectively, fundamental knowledge is needed about loadbearing systems and structures, their advantages and disadvantages and the forces that come into play. These different forces seem complex at first, but they are logically coherent.

It is easiest to explain how they fit together in the order in which they are addressed for a statical calculation. A calculation of this type usually follows these steps:

_ Analysing the overall structure and the function of the individual structural elements in it – statical system
_ Determining all the forces working on the structural elements – assumed loads
_ Calculating the forces affecting a particular structural element and the forces that it transmits to others – calculating the external forces
_ Calculating the forces within the structural element itself – investigating internal or static forces
_ Determining the stability of the planned structural element
_ Proof that the planned structural element can withstand the forces determined

FORCES

$F = m \cdot a$

Force is defined as mass times acceleration.

Newton

The unit used for measuring force is the newton; a newton corresponds roughly to the weight of 100 grammes. In building the newton is complemented by the kilonewton and the meganewton.

Kilonewton:
$1 \text{ kN} = 1000 \text{ N}$,
Meganewton:
$1 \text{ MN} = 1,000,000 \text{ N}$ > Fig. 1

A force is determined by magnitude and direction. Its action is linear, and is expressed by its line of application and the direction of this line.

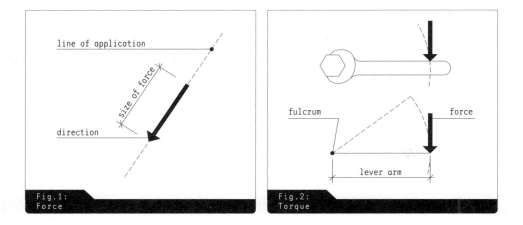

Fig.1:
Force

Fig.2:
Torque

Moments,
torque

Forces can also work in a circle around a point. They are then called torque or moments, and are defined by their size multiplied by the distance from the fulcrum (lever arm).

A simple example of torque is tightening a screw with a screwdriver. This also demonstrates the link between force magnitude and lever arm. The longer the lever arm, the greater the torque. › Fig. 2

Action =
reaction

Statics describes the distribution of forces in a system at rest. Buildings or parts of buildings are usually motionless, and all the effective forces balance each other out. This can be summed up in the law "action = reaction". It is used as a starting point in statical calculations, on the basis that the sum of all forces in any one direction and its counter-direction is zero. If the action is known, the reaction can be determined immediately. The chapter External forces, Support forces explains the methods that apply this possible to loadbearing systems.

STATICAL SYSTEM

A structural engineer first establishes the connections within the construction in the statical system. A statical system is an abstract model of the real, complex structure of the component parts. Supporting members are considered as lines even if they have a wide cross section, and their load is treated as a point. Walls are presented as disc structures and their loads are applied in lines. Additional information the statical system gives is how the structural elements are joined together, and how their forces are distributed from one element to another. This is crucial to the calculations. The symbols used in statical systems are explained in the chapter External forces, Support forces › Fig. 8, p. 16 and are used subsequently in the text.

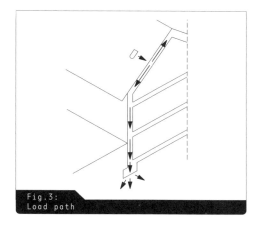

Fig.3:
Load path

Positions

The next working stage involves identifying all the structural elements in sequence as positions and numbering them. Here it is also important to establish which structural elements load which others.

Load path

For example, roof tiles are not just supported by the roof structure, but also affect the walls, right down to the foundations. It must be established with absolute precision which structural elements absorb the loads from the upper storeys. › Fig. 3

EXTERNAL FORCES

If we consider a building element such as a roof beam, we distinguish between two types of force. First, there are the forces exerted on it by the roof structure above it, and those that it transfers to the masonry supporting it. If we do not consider its dead weight, it does not matter in the first

\\ Tip:
For good cooperation with structural engineers, it is important that designers be familiar with these specialists' part of the work in a project and understand their working methods and aims. It therefore makes sense to look at their calculations and positional and working plans and compare them with the architect's documents. After the structural engineer has devised the structure with the architect in the design phase, the main thrust of his or her work is to draw up the statics for planning permission and later to draw the plans for constructing the shell. Here the interest is above all in the loadbearing parts of a building. All the non-loadbearing elements, even non-loadbearing walls, for example, are only significant as loads, and may not feature in the plans at all.

place whether this beam is thick or thin, weak or strong, as we are dealing with external forces that do not include the beam itself.

We must distinguish between external forces and the internal forces operating in the beam itself. For example, how great is the bending force in the roof beam exerted by the roof construction it supports? This bending moment is one of the internal forces that will be explained in the corresponding chapter.

Actions

Everything that can affect a structural element is called an action. Actions are usually forces with different causes. Forces that affect structural elements mechanically are also called loads.

Loads

Loads affect structural elements from the outside, and we must distinguish between them and the reaction forces explained in the subsection Support forces. Loads are divided into various categories. We distinguish between point, line and area loads, according to the degree of abstraction of the statical system. › Fig. 4

In addition, we distinguish between constant, variable and extraordinary actions, in relation to the duration of the action.

Permanent loads

Constant action includes, above all, the weight forces of the structural elements, called permanent loads.

Working loads

The working loads include the variable actions wind, snow and ice loads. Working loads have to be planned in at standard levels for the building's intended use. The most important are the vertical working loads that must be worked out for floors. Whether the rooms are for homes, offices, meeting rooms or some other purpose, they must be given an appropriate working load value as an area load. Largely horizontally applied loads also have to be taken into account, such as loads on railings and parapets, braking, acceleration and collision loads for vehicles, dynamic loads for machines, and earthquake loads. The size of these loads is fixed in national standards, which give them in tables. › Appendix, Literature

Assumed loads

After using the statical system to explain how the structure functions, the next step is to determine the actions. All the acting forces must be identified, assigned a value and added together. They are generally related to a metre or square metre of the structural element. Loads acting obliquely are usually divided into a horizontal and a vertical element.

Vertical load
Horizontal load
› ♀

For further calculations we distinguish between vertical loads, horizontal loads and torque.

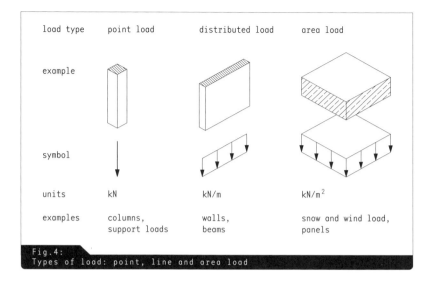

load type	point load	distributed load	area load
example			
symbol			
units	kN	kN/m	kN/m^2
examples	columns, support loads	walls, beams	snow and wind load, panels

Fig. 4:
Types of load: point, line and area load

Load absorption area

Load absorption area describes the particular reference area for loads on a structural element. It is part of an overall surface whose load is being dissipated to a certain structural element. It relates to the nature and span of a structure.

Example: The beams of a timber beam floor are 80 cm apart. Which part of the floor is acting on an individual beam? The load absorption area extends from the middle of the space between the beams on the left-hand side to the middle of the space on the right-hand side, twice 40 cm. So overall it is again 80 cm wide. › Fig. 5 This is a simple example, but determining

\\Important:
Loads acting vertically per square metre in a structural element: dead weight, working loads for floors, stairs, balconies
Acting vertically per square floor plan metre: snow load
Acting at right angles to the area of the structural element: wind load
Generally acting horizontally: loads on parapets and railings, braking and acceleration loads, collision loads from vehicles, earthquake loads

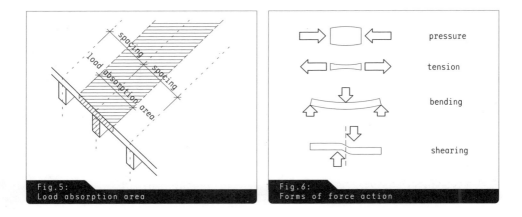

Fig.5:
Load absorption area

Fig.6:
Forms of force action

pressure
tension
bending
shearing

the load absorption area can be more complicated according to the particular structural element.

Force action forms

So far we have considered loads and their magnitude, but how a load, or more generally a force, acts on a structural element is also important. Here we distinguish between the following action forms:

> _ Compression: one stone lies on top of another, exerting pressure on it.
> _ Tension: tensile load is most clearly explained using the example of a rope, which can absorb only tensile forces.
> _ Bending: a beam is fixed at both ends and then loaded from above. It sags, i.e. it is subject to a bending load.
> _ Shearing: this load is explained by the way a pair of household scissors loads paper to cut it. Two forces work on each other slightly offset and transversely to the structural element. This load often acts on connecting devices such as screws. › Fig. 6

Supports

Points of contact between structural elements at which forces are transmitted are called supports. A simple example is a ceiling beam supported on masonry. The beam has its support on the crown of the wall. In building the idea of the support is somewhat broader, and covers many different points of contact between structural elements. For example, when a flagpole is fixed into the ground or a steel beam is connected to a steel

Fig.7:
Supports in steel construction

column, this is also called a support. In terms of structural engineering they differ primarily in the forces that they can dissipate.

It is very easy to look at the different forms of supports in old steel bridges. Large bridge girders are supported on very small points or narrow strips. This means that the girders can deflect without interference from the supports, which are then known as <u>articulated supports</u>. These are used on one side of the bridge, while those on the other side are additionally supported by steel rollers.

When the bridge girders expand with heat, the supports move on these rollers in order to compensate for the difference in length. Bearings of this kind can absorb the vertical forces affecting the bridge, but do not resist horizontal forces such as those caused by expansion movement as a result of temperature change, and they do not prevent the girders from deflecting either. For this reason they are called expansion bearings.

These supports are not on rollers and thus transfer horizontal as well as vertical forces. They are known as fixed bearings or simply <u>articulations</u>.

What happens to the above-mentioned flagpole fixed into the ground? Its anchorage can transfer vertical and horizontal forces from the mast into the ground, and thus also prevent the mast from tipping over – a turning movement around the support. A support of this kind is called a restraint. › Fig. 8

We distinguish between three forms of support:

_ <u>Simple supports</u> can dissipate forces from one direction only. They slide and are articulated.

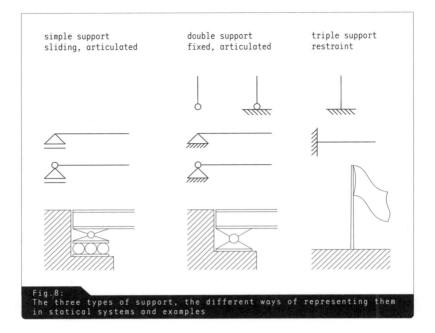

Fig.8:
The three types of support, the different ways of representing them in statical systems and examples

simple support
sliding, articulated

double support
fixed, articulated

triple support
restraint

_ Double supports can absorb forces from several directions. They are fixed and articulated.

_ Restraints are triple supports and can absorb forces from different directions, as well as moments.

The correct choice of support is very important in construction, and must therefore be represented in statical systems. › **Chapter Statical systems**

Support forces

Let us assume that a beam is supported on a spiral spring rather than masonry. The spring is compressed by the load from the beam, thus creating a counter-force to the load that the beam exerts.

This force is called support reaction. › Fig. 9 If the beam does not move, the reaction force of the spring is exactly the same as the force exerted by the beam. Put simply: action equals reaction. › Fig. 10 It is not possible to see this in the masonry that usually provides support, but it is compressed just like the spring, so that it can generate the support reaction force.

When calculating a construction it is necessary to know the magnitude of the forces that the supports have to apply to support the structural element above them. The support forces are therefore always calculated

Support
reaction

16

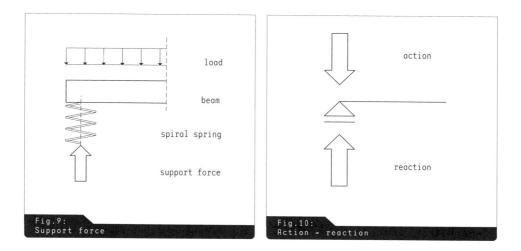

Fig. 9:
Support force

Fig. 10:
Action = reaction

immediately after investigating the loads. Applying the above-mentioned law that action = reaction, it is possible to set up three theses for each structural element that make it possible to calculate the support forces. These three principles are the fundamental tools for statical calculations.

Conditions for
equilibrium

They are also known as the three conditions for equilibrium: › Fig. 11

$$\sum V = 0$$

All vertical loads together are the same as all the vertical support reactions. This means: the sum of all vertical forces equals zero.

$$\sum H = 0$$

All horizontal loads together are the same as all the horizontal support reactions. This means: the sum of all horizontal forces equals zero.

$$\sum M_P = 0$$

If a support is considered at a support point P, all the forces turning clockwise around this point are the same as all the forces turning anti-clockwise. This means: the sum of all moments around the given point equals zero. Here it should be noted that any force or load can be seen as a torsional force around a fixed point, so by definition the force times the lever arm length gives the size of the torsional force. › Chapter Forces

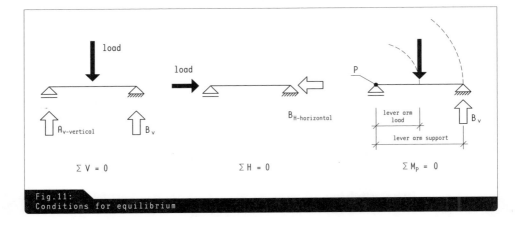

It is only by working out the sum of moments around a support that it becomes possible to calculate two different support forces. Because the torque centre is in a support, the support force does not have a lever there and equals zero in this equation. This means there is only one unknown in the calculation, and that is the other support force, which can be calculated easily.

So for the beams shown in Figure 11 with a single central load the sum of the torque around point P is as follows:

$$\sum \widehat{M}_A = 0 = A_v \cdot 0 + F \cdot l/2 - B_v \cdot l \rightarrow B_v = \frac{F \cdot l}{l \cdot 2} \rightarrow \quad B_v = F/2$$

Both supports dissipate half the central single load. This conclusion could have been reached without calculation in this case.

A rule of signs has to be decided for all calculations using the conditions for equilibrium. Rules of signs are not defined and so the statement must always be represented with an arrow. It shows the direction of the forces that are treated as positive. In this case turning to the right was treated as positive, so left-hand forces must be stated with a negative rule of signs.

INTERNAL FORCES

So far we have discussed only the forces impacting on a structural element and the forces the support generates as a reaction to them. These are called external forces, because the structural element itself has not yet

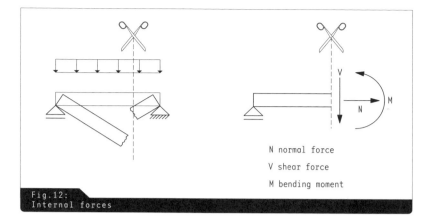

N normal force

V shear force

M bending moment

Fig.12:
Internal forces

been considered. But what is happening in the beam itself, or put another way, what forces are effective in the member?

To understand this, imagine a beam on two supports is cut through at a random point. What happens? It collapses and cannot support anything, not even itself. The crucial question now is what forces have to be effective at this cut face to prevent the beam from falling, or what forces are needed in order to achieve an internal equilibrium of forces.

Here the above-mentioned conditions for equilibrium are useful, as they apply equally to internal and external forces. It is assumed that the external forces acting from the plane of the cut to the end of the beam have to be as great as the internal forces that counteract the external ones at the plane of the cut. › Fig. 12

Internal focus   Just as the external forces are identified as vertical forces, horizontal forces and torque, internal forces are identified as <u>normal forces</u>, <u>shear forces</u> and <u>bending moments</u>, and their direction always relates to the structural element itself.

Normal force

A normal force is a force working longitudinally or in the direction of a structural element. As the first example illustrating a normal force we will take a rope hanging on a hook, with a weight attached to the rope. › Fig. 13 The weight is the load and the hook provides the support reaction. These would be the external forces.

Tensile force   Leaving out the weight of the rope itself, the same tensile force is effective at every point in the rope. Here it does not matter whether the rope is short or long. Therefore the same normal force is effective

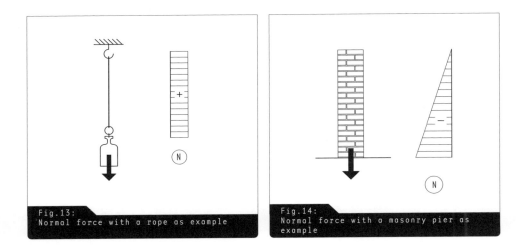

Fig.13:
Normal force with a rope as example

Fig.14:
Normal force with a masonry pier as example

at every point in the rope, and its magnitude is the weight of the weight attached.

Two longitudinal directions of forces were explained in the section Force action forms: pressure and tension. This is a tensile force.

We take a free-standing masonry pier for our next example. › Fig. 14 The pier's dead weight is the only load identified: masonry is a heavy material. It is easy to calculate the support reaction of the foundation at the base of the pier, as this must be the same as the weight of the pier. But what happens in the pier itself? The topmost stone takes no load from any other, so there is no normal force at this point. The second stone from the top takes the load of the one above it. So at the point of the second stone from the top there is a small normal force in the form of a compression force. This compression force becomes greater stone course by stone course to the bottom of the pier. That is to say, the normal force increases from the top to the bottom of the pier. › Chapter Forces

The magnitude of the normal force can be demonstrated in diagrams, similarly to the representation of loads. The two examples show different flows of normal forces. In diagrams of this kind, tensile forces are noted with positive signs and compression forces with negative signs. › Figs 13 and 14

Compression force

Sheer force

For external forces, a distinction is made between horizontal and vertical forces. Internal forces have the same relationship, but their direction relates to the system axis of the member in each case. Just as the longitudinally effective tensile and compression forces are defined as nor-

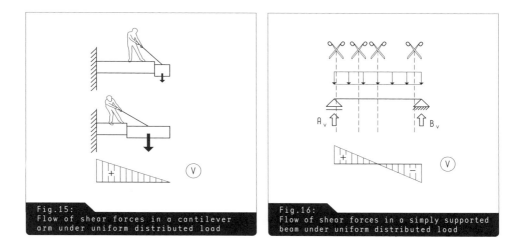

mal forces, all the forces working transversely to them are known as shear forces. They are not as easy to understand as normal forces, and must not be confused with bending, which is explained in the next chapter.

Cantilever arm

The effect of shear force will be explained taking a cantilever arm as example. Figure 15 shows a beam that is fixed into a wall at one end. This kind of beam is known as a cantilever arm. It could be part of a balcony, for example, and is loaded by its dead weight as a uniform distributed load. If this beam were cut through close to its end, the section cut off would fall because of this distributed load. The load works transversely to the axis of the member and thus produces the shear force. If a longer piece is cut off, more of the uniform distributed load has to be absorbed as a force transverse to the member axis at that point. Thus the shear force is greater at this point than at the previous one. The force would increase with every additional cut. The shear force thus increases from its free end towards the fixing point. So the support force at the point of fixing must be able to react to this shear force equally.

Simply supported beam

Figure 16 considers a beam on two supports, called a simply supported beam, with a uniform distributed load. The simplest thing to understand is the flow of shear forces when imagining one section after another cut off from left to right and considering what external forces are at work to the left of the cutting face.

The first interesting cutting face is just to the right of the support on the left. What happens in this section? The support force from the support is exerted upwards transversely to the member axis. Thus the shear force corresponds to the support force. But if a further cut is made to the right, part of the line force works in the other direction. This reduces the shear force in relation to the previous result.

Now a cut is made precisely in the middle. What forces are working transversely to the member from its left-hand end to the cutting plane? They are, first, the support force towards the top, and then the distributed load of the member section from the left-hand end to the centre. So half the distributed load of the entire member is effective. In a symmetrical system like this one it is easy to establish that each support dissipates half the distributed load. In this case the shear force in the middle of the beam equals zero.

If we now consider another cutting face to the right of this, an even greater proportion of the line force is effective. This means that the shear force becomes negative. At the cutting face just in front of the left-hand support almost the whole distributed load is working against the unchanged support force of the left-hand support. It is only the support force of the right-hand support that makes the result add up to zero again.

If the right-hand section of the beam had been considered instead of the left, the result would have been the same. So it does not matter which subsystem is considered, as the internal forces have to be in equilibrium at every point in the beam. This applies to all internal forces.

Bending moment

The effect of moments has already been discussed in the chapter External forces. Here all the effective forces were seen as turning around a fixed point. Their magnitude is defined as force times lever arm. › Chapters Forces and External forces, Support forces While the support forces were interesting for the external forces, the forces working in the run of the beams are important for determining the internal moments.

Bending

The internal moments cause the beam to bend. Bending is the key load for which many structural elements have to be dimensioned. When making statical calculations it is therefore necessary to know how great the bending moments need to be at any given point in the beam. This is shown in the moment gradient, which is thus an important aid for constructing members under bending load.

The direct link between internal moment and bending will again be explained below using a cantilever arm. How does the cantilever arm deform under a uniform distributed load? The load causes the beam to bend downwards. ›Fig. 17 Here, deformation through bending means that the beam has to become longer at the top and short at the bottom. This creates a tensile force at the stretched top side and a compression force at the squashed bottom side. These tensions counteract the load as an internal force.

Thus the bending itself creates the internal moments whose magnitude depends on the magnitude of the external forces and the length of

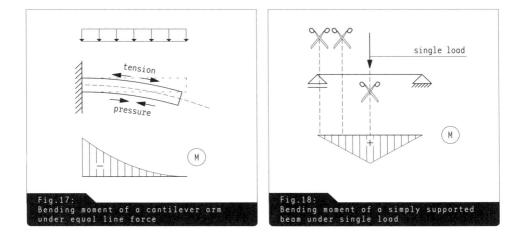

their lever arm. For the cantilever beam there is low distributed load with a low lever arm force at the free end, and the moment is consequently small. But at the fixing point the full distributed load is effective, with a great lever arm force, so the moment is large. › Fig. 17

A simply supported beam under a single load will deflect downwards. Thus, in contrast to the cantilever arm described above, it will be stretched at the bottom and squashed at the top.

Here the bending is in a different direction from the previous example. How does this affect the flow of forces? Let us examine the beam from left to right.

The support force is effective at the right side of the left support, but it has no lever arm force, so the bending moment is zero. As the lever arm force increases with distance from the support, the moment increase is linear. This is the case up to the point where the single load is exerted. To the right of this, the single load works against the support force with increasing lever arm force, and the bending force diminishes until it becomes zero again at the second support. This test can be carried out as from the left-hand or the right-hand side as desired; the result is the same in each case. › Fig. 18

How does the flow of forces change if a uniform line force q is being exerted, rather than an individual load? A distributed load can be summed up as a resulting single load whose line of action lies at the centre of gravity of the distributed load. The magnitude of this resulting individual load is force per unit of length times its effective length.

$$R = \frac{q \cdot l \, [\text{kN} \cdot \text{m}]}{\text{m}}$$

To calculate the bending moments, these resultant individual loads and their lever arm lengths have to be established at the various cutting

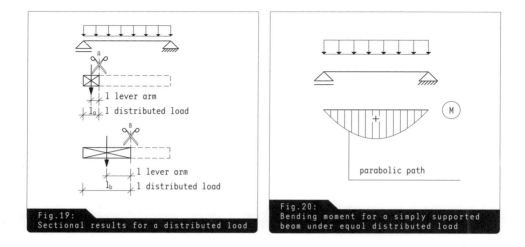

Fig.19:
Sectional results for a distributed load

Fig.20:
Bending moment for a simply supported beam under equal distributed load

planes. › Fig. 19 These act against the support force with increasing magnitude. The resultant moment gradient is a parabola, because the length as that of the distributed load and that of the lever arm goes into the calculation twice.

Moment of a distributed load: $M_A = q \cdot l \cdot l/2 \rightarrow M_A = \dfrac{q \cdot l^2}{2}$

The supports are important points for the moment gradient, and the bending force is again zero at both. How can this be explained? If we make a cut at the support and look in the direction of the support › Fig. 19 no force has a lever arm, because the member has no measurable length here; we are actually looking at a point. In general it can be said that bending requires a fixed beam cross section that can resist moments. But this does not apply if a cut is made in an articulated joint, which a hinged support is. A chain, for example, is an accumulation of articulated joints, and therefore cannot absorb bending. Hence we have an important principle: the bending moment in an articulated joint is zero. › Fig. 20

Maximum moment

In this example, the greatest moment is in the centre of the span. To bear loads, the beam must be able to resist this greatest moment. It is true in general that when dimensioning a structural element, the bending, the location and value of the maximum moment must be established.

When planning elaborate beams over large spans, the maximum moment is not the only important factor. It can be economical in terms of material to adapt the cross section of the beam to the moment gradient, in other words to shape the beam so that it is dimensioned precisely for the bending moment effective at every point. For this reason an architect should be able to determine the moment gradient in a beam qualitatively appropriately to the load.

Correspondence between the internal forces

The three different internal forces are introduced in the above paragraphs. When calculating loadbearing structures it is generally necessary to establish all three internal forces, so that a structural element can be dimensioned to deal with all three working together.

Shear force and moment correspond closely above and beyond this. The two forces, which result from the same load, permit inferences to be drawn from each other. For example, if no force is acting around a rod, the value of the shear force cannot change either, i.e. it is constant. But because moments are defined as force times lever arm, their changes of magnitude in an unloaded area are linear. If a force is acting at the place in question, the values of the resultant moment change in proportion to its distance from that place. Such interrelationships between shear force path and moment gradient are inevitable. › Fig. 21

The following correspondence in particular is important for statical calculations: if we compare the force flows, it becomes clear that the shear force has a zero crossover at the locations of the maximum moments. This turns out to be useful, because the location of the maximum moment can be ascertained from the flow of shear forces, and then has to be calculated at this point only. › Figs 21 and 22

And with a little experience, it is also possible to determine the anticipated shear force flow and moment gradient qualitatively. Figure 23 shows the appropriate force flows for some common load types.

1. If no force is effective in the member path, the flow of shear forces is constant and the moment gradient linear.
2. A single line creates a break in the flow of shear forces and a kink in the moment gradient.
3. For uniform distributed loads the flow of shear forces is a sloping straight line and the moment gradient a parabola.

🛈

\\ Hint:

Signs for representing internal forces are fixed as follows:
Normal force: Pressure (–) is represented upwards, pressure (+) downwards.
Shear force: The positive shear force is drawn above, the negative below the system line.

Bending moment: The moments are drawn in the direction of their deflection, the positive moments downwards and the negative ones upwards. But these conventions should not be seen as definitive. For example, some countries represent the bending moments the other way round.

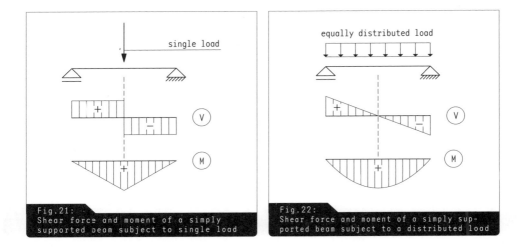

Fig.21:
Shear force and moment of a simply supported beam subject to single load

Fig.22:
Shear force and moment of a simply supported beam subject to a distributed load

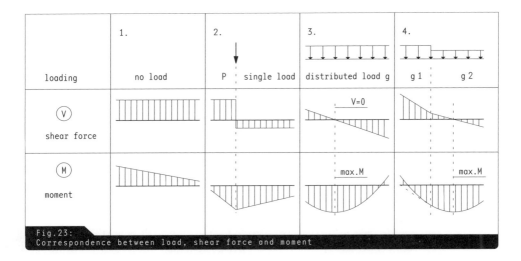

Fig.23:
Correspondence between load, shear force and moment

4. A break in the uniform distributed loads creates a kink in the flow of horizontal forces; in the moment gradient two parabolas with different inclines fit together with the result that they have the same tangents. Columns 1 and 2 in the table could be details from a system as in Figure 21, while Figure 22 can serve as an example for column 3.

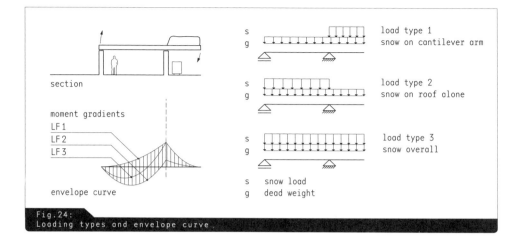

section

moment gradients
LF 1
LF 2
LF 3

envelope curve

s
g   load type 1
    snow on cantilever arm

s
g   load type 2
    snow on roof alone

s
g   load type 3
    snow overall

s   snow load
g   dead weight

Fig.24:
Loading types and envelope curve

Loading types

In practice, many different loads overlap. They have to be added together in the calculation in order to dimension the structural elements for the maximum loading. But there are also cases where danger does not derive from the maximum load. Maximum values for internal forces, which are crucial to the dimensioning, are also possible for other load combinations. These different combinations of loads are called loading types.

Take the following example: a small workshop has a flat timber beam roof with a canopy protruding extensively on one side for the storage of material. A great deal of snow then falls in the winter. As the workshop is well heated and the roof poorly insulated, the snow on the roof melts, but not on the canopy, which has unheated space beneath it. The snow remains on the canopy alone. This load presents the risk of the workshop roof rising, and the roof beams above the wall next to the protruding section breaking. › Fig. 24

To avert these dangers, the structural engineer must calculate not only the snow load for the building as a whole, but the snow load on the canopy as well, as they each introduce different risks. The first step must be to establish what combinations or types of load are possible, and put them together. If the moment gradients of the different load types are then mapped onto each other, the possible extreme value for each point can then be read off from this diagram.

Envelope curve

This figure is also called an envelope curve. Its extremity shows the load type that is crucial for each point. Figure 24 shows that the greatest positive moment in the span occurs in load case 2, but the greatest negative moment in load types 1 and 3.

DIMENSIONING

A statical calculation runs similarly to the sequence in the above chapters. After the statical system has been established, the assumed loads are calculated and then the external forces, and after that the internal forces determined for the component parts of the building.

It would be wonderful if we could now simply work out the required cross section for the element. Unfortunately this is not as simple as it sounds, as all the parts of the building become part of the calculation themselves, as loads; in other words, all the structural elements have to be known in order to work out the assumed loads, so that their weight can be included. If the calculation then reveals that one of the structural elements assessed will not bear sufficient load, we have to start again from the beginning.

Even if this does not mean that all the work is invalidated, careful planning is clearly advantageous at this point: dimensions should be estimated in advance. This can be done with the aid of rough formulae. › Appendix, Pre-dimensioning formulae

Strength

After the forces coming into play have been determined, the load-bearing capacity of the structural elements is now of interest. This depends mainly on two aspects, the material and the cross section.

One of the first steps in designing a construction is to decide on the materials. Every building material has its advantages and disadvantages. The strength or resistance offered by different materials is particularly important for construction. Cable constructions, for example, resist tension but not compression, while masonry resists compression but not tension. Timber, steel and reinforced concrete constructions are compression- and tension-resistant, and also resist internal forces. › Chapter External Forces, Force action forms

It has already been established that compression and tension are both produced by bending. Consequently, only materials that resist both loads can be used when bending loads come into play (e.g. timber and steel members).

Tension

$$\sigma = \frac{F\,[kN]}{A\,[m^2]}$$

Robert Hooke, 1635–1703

Materials also differ in their capacity to absorb forces. This capacity is expressed as the amount of force a material can absorb over a given area. The strength per area is expressed as tension σ.

To understand the concept of resistance we must cite <u>Hooke's Law</u>, which states that tensions and extensions are proportional in the elastic field. What does this mean for building materials? Every material, whether it is wood, steel, reinforced concrete or masonry, is essentially elastic. If a structural element is loaded, tensions are created, causing the material to extend proportionately. So if a beam is loaded, it deflects, or sags. If the load is doubled, it deflects to twice the previous extent. If the load is reduced again the deflection also decreases.

This simple pattern applies only up to a certain point. If the tension becomes too great, the material no longer responds elastically, but plastically, i.e. permanent deformations occur. This is the point at which the structural element starts to be damaged. If it has to take a further load, it fails completely, although the failure differs in kind from material to material. The value indicating how much tension a material can absorb before it deforms plastically and fails is a purely material characteristic and has nothing to do with the geometry of the structural element. It is important for construction that the maximum admissible value is not reached at the highest possible load. The tensions a particular material can absorb are established under laboratory conditions, taking variations in material quality into consideration.

Admissible
tension

The value established in this way is known as admissible tension and can be ascertained from tables. › Appendix, Literature

Strength
classes

In addition, every material is available in different qualities with a variety of admissible tensions, and is assigned to a "strength class". For example, normal and high-strength concretes are distinguished by their strength class. The actual verification of a structural element's loadbearing capacity always works on the principle that the actual tensions must be less than the admissible tensions. The admissible tensions can be established from tables, but the main part of the work is in working out the actual tensions. If structural elements are loaded normally, working these tensions out is simple. The existing tension corresponds to the normal force per sectional area of the structural element. If the result shows that the existing tension is lower than the admissible tension, the structural element is correctly dimensioned. Unfortunately this simple verification is only rarely the deciding factor for dimensioning. Cables, which in fact can absorb only tensile forces, are dimensioned in this way, but in most cases the bending load is the key factor for dimensioning.

Moment resistance

Every proof of suitability for a structural element is based on the actual tensions being lower than the admissible tensions. This also applies to members subject to bending loads.

Stress
distribution

When explaining the bending moment we stated that a bending member is subject to tensile stresses on one side and compression stresses on the other, but how great are these stresses, and how exactly are they distributed?

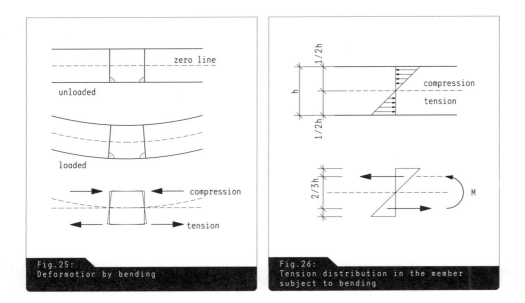

Fig. 25:
Deformation by bending

Fig. 26:
Tension distribution in the member subject to bending

To find this out, consider an unloaded member marked transversely with straight lines. If it deflects when a load is applied, the marks incline towards each other in a trapezoid shape, but the lines remain straight. › Fig. 25 If the extensions and tensions are proportional, this results in a stress distribution that is also in straight lines from the tensile stress at the lower edge via the middle level, which is tension-free, to the compression stress at the upper edge.

Neutral tension plane

As can be seen in Figure 26, the compression and tension distributions each form a triangle. These triangular tensions can each be summed up in a resulting tension at the centre of gravity of the triangle, with a distance from each other of 2/3 of the height of the cross section. This length represents the lever arm of the internal moments that counteract the loads and are thus responsible for loadbearing capacity. So the greater the height of the member, the longer the lever arm of the internal tensions, and the greater the stability of the member.

Thus, the length of this lever arm is the key to resistance to bending, but the section width is also important. This section resistance is expressed as moment resistance. Moment resistance is a value relating to the geometry of a member and not to its material.

For example, the rectangular cross section customary in timber construction produces the moment resistance W with a magnitude of $W = w \cdot h^2 / 6$.

It is worth looking more closely at this formula: the height h is squared, while the width w is simply entered as a factor. An upright rectangular section has a higher loadbearing capacity than a square one, or a horizontal rectangle. Expressed more precisely, doubling the width of a profile doubles the loadbearing capacity, but doubling its height multiplies it by four.

The moment resistance for dimensioning a simply rectangular cross section can be established by using the formula above. For other cross sections, for all steel profiles, for example, the dimensioning is more complicated. For this reason, moment resistance values are always given in sets of tables. › Appendix, Literature

The term moment resistance contains the word moment. In contrast with the concept of moment or torque explained in the chapter Forces, moment resistance refers not to an individual force with a particular lever arm, but to area elements and their lever arm around the tension zero line, as we are considering a cross section area. › Fig. 26 Like moment of inertia, explained in the following chapter, moment resistance is also defined as an area moment.

Moment of inertia

Moment of inertia is best explained by its effect. Moment resistance expresses a member profile's resistance to bending moments, while the moment of inertia relates to its deflection. It describes the rigidity of a cross section.

Like moment resistance, moment of inertia is based on the distribution of tension in a cross section subject to bending. Here the severely compressed and extended areas at the edge are more effective than those in the zero tension line area. But the distance of the area elements from the zero line is more important for moment of inertia than moment resistance.

The moment of inertia is the sum of all area elements in the cross section multiplied by the square of their distance from the zero line.

The moment of inertia for rectangular cross sections is calculated using the formula $I = w \cdot h^3 / 12$. So here the cross section height is raised to the power of three, which means that deflection is reduced by one eighth if the member height is doubled and the width remains the same.

Deflection   Moment of inertia can be used to calculate the expected deflection of a member. Even though the priority is to dimension structural elements for loadbearing capacity through moment resistance, evidence is additionally needed that an admissible maximum deflection is not being exceeded.

Shear stress

Let us take the following example to explain shear stress: two planks are laid one on top of the other as a simply supported beam, and a load

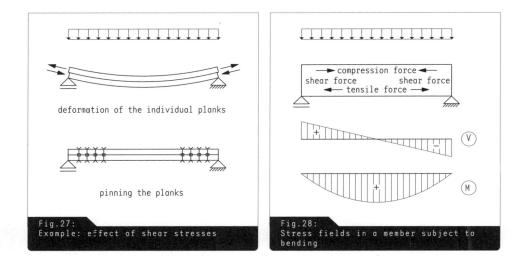

Fig.27:
Example: effect of shear stresses

Fig.28:
Stress fields in a member subject to bending

is then exerted on them. Both planks will deflect under the load and shift in relation to each other. › Figs 27 and 28 They should be fastened together to increase their loadbearing capacity, as a tall cross section has a higher loadbearing capacity than two planks on top of one another with the same height. › Chapter Dimensioning, Moment resistance and Moment of inertia What is the best thing to do?

One possibility could be to drill through the unloaded planks and fasten them together with bolts and dowel pins.

But now we have to ask what stresses these dowel pins are actually expected to absorb and how they come into play. The answer to the first part of the question is simple. Shear stresses are responsible for the planks' shift in position. The simplest way to explain where these stresses come from is by means of the members shown in Figure 28.

In this member subject to a uniformly distributed load the greatest tensile stress is in the middle of the span on its lower side and the greatest compression stress on its upper side. These stresses reduce as the bending moment decreases towards the supports, but what happens to the stresses that cannot just simply disappear? The compression and tensile stresses cancel each other out towards the supports and this happens as a result of the shear stresses that increase as the bending stresses decrease.

The bending stresses can be discerned in the moment gradient, while the shear stresses are proportional to the shear forces and in the case of a member subject to a simple and uniform load the shear forces increase towards the supports. › Chapter Internal forces, Shear force

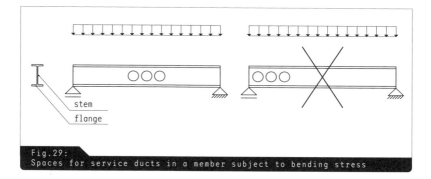

Fig.29:
Spaces for service ducts in a member subject to bending stress

It is essentially true of members of this kind that the tensions resulting from bending in the centre of the span are greatest at the top and bottom of the section › Chapter Internal forces, Bending moment and the maximum shear stresses are at the supports. Timber, for example, is a material that is sensitive to shear stresses. In timber structures it is often necessary to reinforce members to absorb shear stresses at the supports.

I-beam section

Another example is offered here to clarify shear stresses further. The usual steel sections, such as I-beam sections, are designed so that the flanges can absorb the bending compression and bending tension, while the stem absorbs the shear stresses.

For example, if an architect wants holes for wiring or pipework to be cut in a simply supported beam, this does not present a problem in the middle of the beam, as the forces in play tend to be small there, while the two flanges are fully loaded with bending compression and bending tension. But holes should not be drilled near the supports, because here the stem is heavily loaded with shear stresses. › Fig. 29

\\Tip:
The cabling and ducts for power, water, sewage disposal and, above all, ventilation can have a crucial effect on the design of a loadbearing structure. They should be fixed at an early stage and agreed with the structural engineer. Essentially, loadbearing structure and service pipes and ducts should be planned so that as few crossing points are created as possible.

STRUCTURAL ELEMENTS

CANTILEVER ARM, SIMPLY SUPPORTED BEAM, SIMPLY SUPPORTED BEAM WITH CANTILEVER ARM

Loads and forces were explained in the first chapter using the cantilever arm and the simply supported beam as examples. These two load-bearing systems form the basis for most of the more highly developed and more complex systems. It is worth recapitulating their advantages and disadvantages.

Cantilever arm

A cantilever arm can be compared with a long lever used to lift heavy loads. Consequently the leverage acting at the anchor point is the biggest problem. As can be seen in Figure 30, this is the point of maximum torque and maximum shear force, and the anchor point has to absorb both. This is scarcely feasible in timber construction, as no nailed or screwed joint could do the job unless the anchor point were long enough. But an anchor point in masonry is easily possible, although the danger remains that the long lever could lift masonry even if there is not enough of it above the anchor point. If we look at the moment and shear force gradients, it is clear that a cantilever arm subject to a uniformly distributed load has to be dimensioned for the area around its anchor point, but is thus overdimensioned for the rest of its length. It therefore makes sense, saves material and is customary for a cantilever member to have its height reduced from the anchor point to the free end to correspond with the internal force gradients.

Simply supported beam

The simply supported beam is probably the most common loadbearing system, and it is worth looking at carefully again here. A simple timber, steel or even concrete section with a consistent cross section is normally

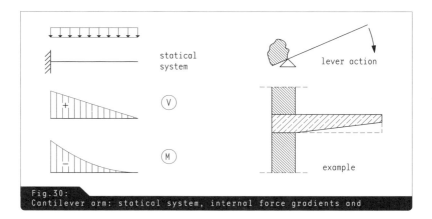

Fig. 30:
Cantilever arm: statical system, internal force gradients and

35

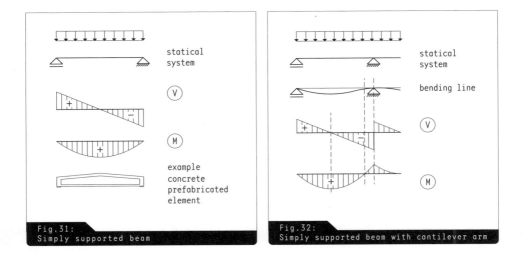

Fig.31:
Simply supported beam

Fig.32:
Simply supported beam with cantilever arm

used, as these are easy to produce and cheap, and also have the advantage of offering a flat surface at the top and the bottom. But actually most simply supported beams are only fully exploited at one point, in the middle, the point of maximum moment. So it can make sense to adapt the beam to the moment gradient and make it higher in the middle than at the supports.
> Fig. 31 and Chapter Internal forces, Bending moment

Wood is a natural product that can absorb considerably fewer forces transversely than it can longitudinally to its grain, and it is thus sensitive to shear forces. In the best cases a timber beam is thus fully exploited at three points, in the middle because of the bending moment and at both ends because of the shear forces. > Chapter Dimensioning, Shear stress

> 🖉
Simply suppor-
ted beam with
cantilever arm

The simply supported beam with cantilever arm is a very useful system from the point of view of loadbearing theory. It could be said that as a combination of the two previous ones it compensates for the disadvantages in each case. The problem with the cantilever arm is its anchor point. But in this system the length of the anchor point, i.e. the span length, is usually greater than the protruding section itself, and thus unproblematic. The key factor for this beam is what happens above the support in the cantilever arm. Here, the cantilever section has its maximum moment, with a negative value. > Fig. 32

A simply supported beam has its maximum positive moment in the middle of the span while at the support it is approaching zero. How do these two lines fit together? This becomes clear if we imagine a member of this kind deflecting when loaded. The cantilever arm would hang down and the member would also sag in the span. It hangs in at the articulated end support, but curves over the other one and lies horizontally over the support.

Bending line

This means that the inflection point of the "bending line" shifts from the support into the span. › Fig. 32

This is also reflected by the moment gradient. Corresponding with the protruding section, the negative maximum lies above the support.

Moment at support

Midspan moment

A negative above a support is called a moment at support. It is not relieved in the span before a "midspan moment" comes into being. This is the term for the positive moment in the area between the supports. Because of the moment at support it is smaller than in the case of a pure simply supported member. The member in the span is thus relieved by the cantilever arm. This means that a member of this kind can be smaller than a simply supported beam over the same span width.

› 🪶

CONTINUOUS BEAM

Continuous beams extend over several spans. They are defined precisely according to the number of these spans. A two-span member has three supports, a three-span member four, and so on. Such systems are a logical extension of the situation explained above. As in the simply supported beam with cantilever arm, a moment at support is created above a central support, and this reduces the bending moments in the spans. Here, the inflection points in the bending line correspond with the zero points in the moment line, although the bending line and the moment line do not have the same form. But the form of the bending line indicates the moment gradient. › Fig. 33 and Chapter Internal forces, Bending moment

So the advantage of continuous members is that they reduce the span moments through the moments at support over the supports. Lower span moments means that the members can be smaller.

✎

\\ Tip:
Squared timber sections used as beams should be neither too slender nor too wide. Sizes with side ratios between 2/3 and 1/3 make sense.
Building tables give timber sections. The section sizes quoted in these tables are usually available from stock in the timber trade, so they do not need to be specially cut to size, which would make additional work for the carpenter.

🪶

\\ Hint:
A positive moment or a midspan moment signifies tensile stress on the bottom side and compression on the top side of the member section. A negative moment or a moment at support creates compression on the top side and pressure on the bottom side (see Chapter Internal forces, Bending moment).

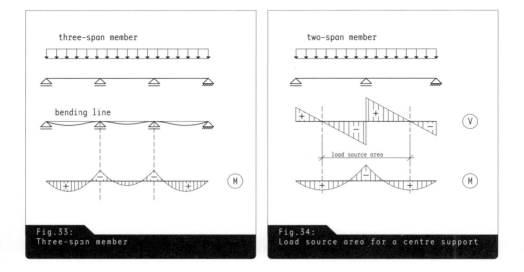

Fig.33:
Three-span member

Fig.34:
Load source area for a centre support

Effect of
continuity
The effect of continuity thus makes significant material savings possible.

Without closer consideration it might well seem that a central support has to bear exactly twice as much load as the peripheral supports. But this is not the case. The threshold of the load source area is not in the middle of the span, but at the point where the shear force is zero and the span moment at its maximum. Thus, a central support takes more than twice the load at a peripheral support. › Fig. 34

ARTICULATED BEAM

Another possibility emerges when looking at the moment gradient of the continuous member: the individual beams can be fitted together at the points of zero moment. This sustains the effect of continuity and, above all, a point of zero moment means that there is no bending at this point.

Point of
zero moment
So if a beam joint is planned for this point, the moment gradient does not change when compared to the continuous beam. In timber construction a beam joint is an articulation, as is the case with almost every nodal point, and the bending moment at an articulated point is inevitably zero. › Figs 35 and 36

Statical
determination
An added articulated joint affects the system in a further way. Continuous beams and articulated beams differ in one essential quality. What happens to a continuous beam if one of the supports is lowered for some reason? The beam will have to bend in order to remain supported by all of them. This creates stresses in the structural member. If this were to happen

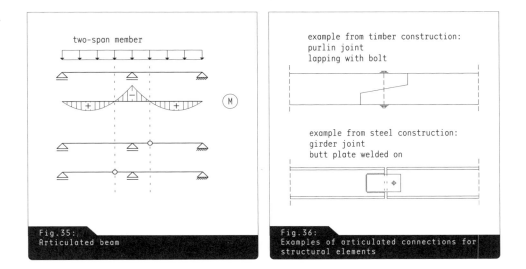

Fig. 35:
Articulated beam

Fig. 36:
Examples of articulated connections for structural elements

to an articulated beam, there would be no stresses in the section, because of the articulated, sliding nature of the support system.

Statically undetermined

Loadbearing structures in which stresses would be created if a support were to be moved are called statically undetermined, and if this does not happen, they are called statically determined. › Fig. 37

Statically determined

For example, cantilever arms and simply supported beams, to which this distinction applies as well, also prove to be statically determined systems. More loadbearing systems will be explained in the following chapters that can be statically determined or statically undetermined. Statical determination always depends on the number and nature of the supports, and the number of articulation points. Adding articulations can turn a statically undetermined system into a statically determined one. But care is needed here, as a superfluous addition would render the system unstable.

Three-span member

Closer consideration of a three-span member with a uniformly distributed load shows that it would need two articulated joints in order to raise or lower each joint without causing stresses. In other words, two articulated joints are needed to make it into a statically determined system. Four points of zero moment show in the moment gradient. There are thus several possibilities for arranging the joints within these points. › Fig. 38

What is the difference between statically determined and undetermined systems in practice? Statically undetermined systems offer a somewhat higher degree of safety based on the distinctions identified above. If, for example, one support for a continuous member should fail, there is

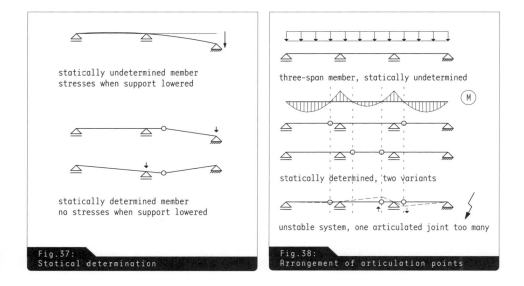

statically undetermined member
stresses when support lowered

statically determined member
no stresses when support lowered

Fig.37:
Statical determination

three-span member, statically undetermined

M

statically determined, two variants

unstable system, one articulated joint too many

Fig.38:
Arrangement of articulation points

a chance that the structural element will not collapse because the member is still supported by the remaining ones. In a statically determined system, such as a simply supported beam, this would not be the case. In addition, statically undetermined systems cannot be calculated using the three conditions for equilibrium. More elaborate calculation methods are needed here.

TRUSSED BEAM

The span width is the most important criterion for choosing a particular loadbearing system. In any construction, it is possible to assign a sensible point for a width at which the span can still function, but will become inefficient if that point is exceeded. For example, this point is reached at approx. 5–6 m for the efficient use of single timber beams. Further measures are needed for wider spans: for example, if it is not possible to place a support underneath, a brace can be inserted instead, › Fig. 39 which will dissipate its load to the supports via a truss. The truss pushes the brace upwards, like a drawn bow, and thus works like a support, even though it does not touch the ground. This system is called a trussed member or beam.

It is also possible to truss a beam doubly or triply. › Fig. 40 This increases the span even further, though the forces in the structural members increase correspondingly. How are the individual parts of the trussed member loaded? The brace is compression loaded, as it is supporting the beam. The truss, which is usually made of steel rods, is subject to a tensile

40

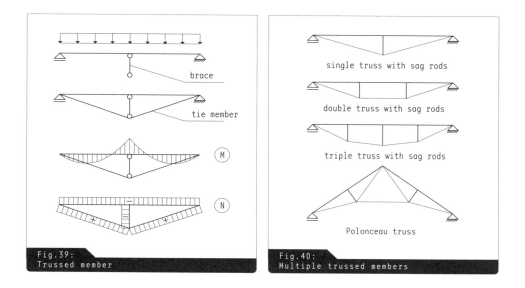

brace

tie member

M

N

single truss with sag rods

double truss with sag rods

triple truss with sag rods

Polonceau truss

Jean B.-C.
Polonceau,
1813–1859

force and the beam, which was originally subject only to a bending load additionally acquires compression as a counterforce to this tensile force.

More complicated systems can be constructed with the aid of braces and trusses. One example is the Polonceau truss, named after its inventor. › Fig. 40

It is possible to sum up what was achieved by the trussed member as follows: the simple beam becomes a complex system that deals with the loads not just by absorbing bending moments, but by dissipating them as compression and tension in various structural elements set at a great distance from each other. The upper member is no longer subject mainly to bending forces, but also to compression, and the truss dissipates the tension forces. When explaining the bending moment, we talked about the lever arm of the compression-loaded cross section parts as opposed to the compression-loaded ones. This lever arm is clearly enlarged here. Hence, such systems are considerably more efficient. › Chapter Dimensioning, Moment resistance

LATTICE

A trussed girder with more than three struts makes less sense for a number of reasons. But if the struts are supported individually in every section, this produces a new system that can cope with considerably larger spans. It is known as a trussed, lattice or skeleton girder. In these lattice girders the tension-loaded sections are usually made up not of cables or

bars, but of timber or steel sections. Lattices are efficient systems that are very common, and can be adapted to fit the requirements of a particular situation. They can be realized in almost any material, and the bars can be arranged in very varied ways. › Fig. 42

In the examples discussed so far, the diagonals have been realized as tension-loaded bars, corresponding to the truss below them. But it is equally possible to install the bars exactly the opposite way round.

They are then compression loaded. To identify the direction of forces in the diagonals, it helps to ask whether they are loaded with compression forces, like an arch, or with tension forces, like a sagging cable.

It is also possible to construct lattice trusses with diagonal members alone, in alternate directions. The look of the truss does not change in the

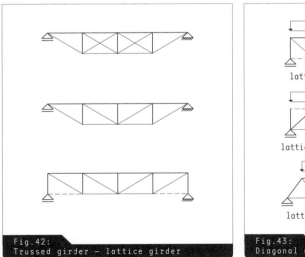

Fig. 42:
Trussed girder – lattice girder

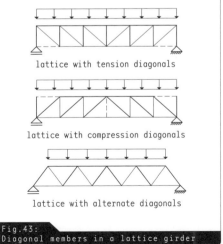

lattice with tension diagonals

lattice with compression diagonals

lattice with alternate diagonals

Fig. 43:
Diagonal members in a lattice girder

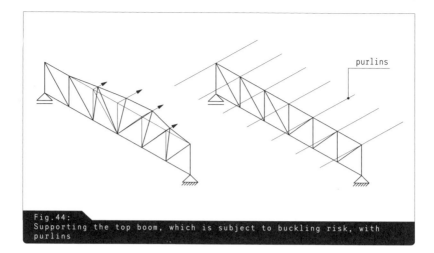

purlins

Fig.44:
Supporting the top boom, which is subject to buckling risk, with purlins

middle. The bars in one direction are compression loaded and the others tension loaded, and in the middle of the lattice structure the sections change their load, while their arrangement remains the same.

Unstrained members

There are individual bars in lattice girders that on closer consideration are not directly involved in dissipating the load. They are neither tension nor compression diagonals, and are thus called unstrained members. Nevertheless, they cannot usually be omitted, because they are needed for structural reasons. This can mean that they complete the outlines of the system or hold it in position. In the figures, compression members are drawn as thick lines, tension members as thin lines and unstrained members as dashed lines. › Fig. 43

The height and length of a lattice girder is calculated according to the span. But its width depends only on the girder section selected in each case, and is usually very narrow in comparison with the overall length. For this reason the compression loaded upper section, called the top boom, is at risk of buckling. › Fig. 44

Top boom

This problem can be solved in a variety of ways.

Purlins

The top boom can be fixed to a ceiling above it or to longitudinal ceiling beams, and thus prevented from moving out of place; or it can be constructed as a buckleproof girder in its own right.

Three boom truss

If a second boom is added to the top boom, which is in danger of buckling, and a kind of lattice is constructed with diagonal braces between the two, this produces a rigid support element in both directions, called a three-boom truss. › Fig. 45

› ✎

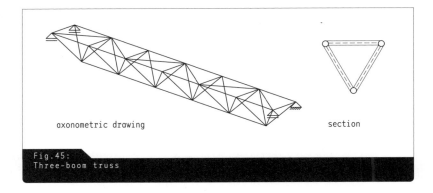

axonometric drawing   section

Fig.45:
Three-boom truss

SLAB

Timber or steel constructions are almost always directional systems, i.e. the bar-shaped sections means that loads are always dissipated in a particular direction. Concrete, however, makes it possible to created statically non-directional, flat structural components.

Reinforced concrete

Fundamentally, the following applies to the loadbearing properties of reinforced concrete: as artificial stone made of cement, water and aggregates such as gravel or chippings, concrete is very good at absorbing compression forces, but like masonry does not absorb tension forces well. It is therefore usually combined with steel.

Reinforcement

In this material structure, the concrete absorbs the compression forces and the steel the tension forces. The previous chapters on the various support types have already explained where tension forces occur in structural components. This is precisely where the reinforcing elements are placed in reinforced concrete, i.e. bar steel is cast in. For slabs, this is usually needed on the undersides and in peripheral areas. If a reinforced concrete slab is used like a continuous girder, steel reinforcement is also built in on the top side. When concreting a floor slab, steel bars are usually inserted in the form of mats welded crosswise, enclosed by concrete on all

\\ Tip:
The nodes in lattice girders should be constructed so that the sections — or more precisely, their centre lines — meet precisely at one point. This avoids generating forces that twist the node and would subject it to additional loading.

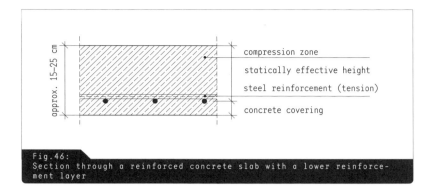

Fig.46:
Section through a reinforced concrete slab with a lower reinforcement layer

sides to be able to support the load compositely. The thickness needed for a concrete floor depends on the span, and is usually 15–25 cm. › Fig. 46

Concrete slabs are almost the only structural components that can be non-directional. Over a square space, a concrete floor can dissipate its loads to all four walls at the same time. But if the floor is rectangular the loads will be dissipated via the short span in the first place, because if the deflection is even it will be more heavily loaded than the long span, thus producing greater tensions. For a concrete floor that is twice as long as it is broad, the proportion of loading absorbed by the long span is scarcely significant. But the reinforcement is not simply fitted to relate to the main direction in which the load is borne. A slab is always reinforced transversely as well, as the flat effect brings its own advantages. This means, for example, that point loads are better distributed, and the forces in the floor remain lower.

The longer the span, the thicker the floor will need to be. But if a floor is thicker than 25 cm, its dead weight becomes so large that it is scarcely viable any longer as a solid flat floor. Strictly speaking, only the upper edge of the floor is effectively involved in dissipating the compression load, and the steel bars dissipate the tension stresses. The rest of the structure is actually just a link, or a filler.

Ribbed floor

If floors are very thick, it makes sense to reduce their dead weight by omitting areas from the lower edge to the effective upper zone. The reinforcement is then placed mainly in ribs, which lie very close to each other. A ribbed floor can thus accommodate much wider spans than a flat one.

Binding joists

Another approach to bridging large spans involves using binding joists. Unlike ribs, binding joists are not seen as part of the floor area, but as beams on which the flat floors will be laid. › Fig. 47 and Fig. 69, p. 63

Slab beams

For concrete structures cast on the building site (in-situ concrete structures), binding joists best use the advantages of the monolithic

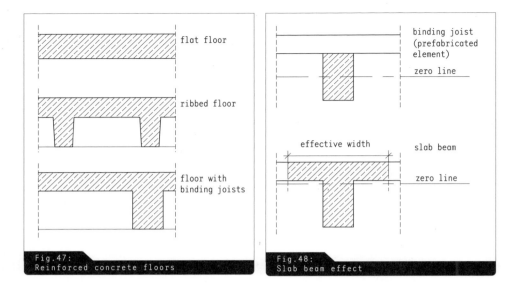

Fig. 47:
Reinforced concrete floors

Fig. 48:
Slab beam effect

construction method. Here, "monolithic" means that all the in-situ concrete elements, even if they have been concreted at different stages, work as a continuous structure. So binding joists exploit not only the static height to the bottom edge of the slab, but also its thickness. Furthermore, the part of the slab by the beam on both sides enlarges the compression zone. In such cases, the term slab beam is used. › Fig. 48

COLUMN

Unlike horizontal loadbearing elements, columns are subject to hardly any bending load, but primarily to normal forces. A very narrow column cross section would suffice for dissipating normal forces if it were not for the danger that the column might sag sideways and fail.

Buckling

Slender columns run the risk of buckling, but the magnitude of this risk depends on various factors. The important features for a column are the loads, the material, and how slender it is. The Swiss mathematician Leonhard Euler (1707–1783) established how the way columns are fixed at the top and bottom affects their buckling properties, and identified four different cases, which are named after him.

Euler cases

The Euler cases set out four ways in which columns can be braced or provided with articulated joints. When buckling, columns adopt the form of a sinus curve. The way the columns are attached affects the length of this sinus curve, or the distance between their inflection points, which is important in its turn for the stability of the column. The length of the

46

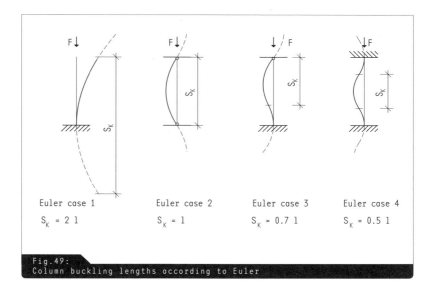

Euler case 1   Euler case 2   Euler case 3   Euler case 4

$S_K = 2\,l$ $S_K = l$ $S_K = 0.7\,l$ $S_K = 0.5\,l$

Fig.49:
Column buckling lengths according to Euler

column in relation to the deformation curve is known as the <u>effective</u> or <u>buckling length</u>.

    Figure 49 shows the four cases with the same column length. Euler case 1 works on the flagpole principle: the deformation curve is very long, which is unfavourable in terms of stability. Euler case 2 relates to a column that is attached by an articulated joint at the top and the bottom. This case is very common, and the deformation curve or buckling length is shorter, which makes the column more stable. In Euler case 3, the column is braced on one side. This bracing stops the column from twisting at that point and thus reduces the length of the sinus curve, i.e. the buckling length. Euler case 4 with bracing at the top and bottom produces the shortest buckling length for the column, and is consequently the most stable variant.

> ⋔

⋔

\\ Hint:
Euler's buckling behaviour for columns assumes
compression- and tensionproof material such
as steel or wood. Euler's scheme is not suitable for dimensioning columns in masonry or
concrete.

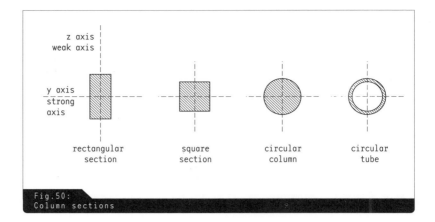

z axis
weak axis

y axis
strong
axis

rectangular
section

square
section

circular
column

circular
tube

Fig.50:
Column sections

Another major factor for dimensioning a column is its slenderness. It is easy to assume that slenderness implies a ratio of column length to its thickness. But this is not the case: thickness is not part of the equation, but its stability as a ratio of moment of inertia and cross section area are; and then again it is not the length of the column, but Euler's buckling length, as explained above, that is crucial. So the slenderness of a column is the ratio of its buckling length to its bending strength.

It is possible to use these factors involved in calculating columns to make a theoretical statement about the best possible shape for them: columns that are loaded only vertically can buckle in any direction. However, they will actually buckle in the direction in which they have the lowest bending strength. So columns should be equally stable in every direction, as would be the case for a square or – even better – a circular column.

In addition, bending strength in relation to the moment of inertia makes it possible to draw further conclusions about the ideal cross section. With respect to the distribution of tensions in a buckling column it is clear that the areas some distance away from the plane of zero tension or the centre are the most effective. In tubes, the less effective central areas are omitted. Here the material is placed as far away as possible from the central point. This suggests that a tube, and ideally a round tube, is the best possible shape for a column. This deduction is highly theoretical, and is intended only to explain the loading on a column, as ultimately a lot of other factors influence their structure, and all these have to be taken into consideration. > Figs 50 and 51

Fig.51:
Columns

CABLE

Cables do not obey any of the rules explained in previous chapters. If a cable is part of a loadbearing structure, it sags according to the load suspended on it or its own weight, and changes its form with every change of load. It cannot resist bending moments, and always takes up the form in which no moment occurs anywhere. This form corresponds precisely with the bending moment of a girder, rather than a cable.

Funicular line   So the "funicular line" corresponds with the cable's moment curvature. › Fig. 52

A second important difference from the loadbearing structures discussed previously is the fact that cable loadbearing structures always have horizontal reactions at the support as well. Cables dissipate all loads as normal forces, i.e. the funicular force, and correspondingly the horizontal reaction force, follow the direction of the cable at the support exactly. Only if the cable were hanging vertically would the reaction at support be verti-

Sag   cal alone. › Fig. 13, p. 20 In Figure 53, comparing the two cables shows that the vertical proportion of the funicular force corresponding to the magnitude of the loads remains the same, while the horizontal proportion changes with the angle of the cable, i.e. with its slack.

Funicular force   Something we have all experienced with a tight or slack washing line is an important factor for all cable loadbearing structures: a low sag level means a high funicular force, and a high sag level a low funicular force.

So why are they not used much more often? Cable-stayed structures have their vagaries in practical applications. The magnitude of the deformations they admit causes great difficulties in built structures. Uncontrolled movements – flapping in the wind, for example – have to be completely suppressed in order to avoid large dynamic stresses. Cable-stayed

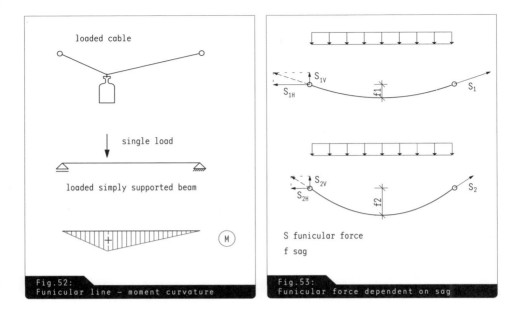

loaded cable

single load

loaded simply supported beam

(M)

Fig.52:
Funicular line – moment curvature

S_{1V}
S_{1H}
S_1
f1

S_{2V}
S_{2H}
S_2
f2

S funicular force
f sag

Fig.53:
Funicular force dependent on sag

structures therefore have to be stable in form in every case, which few methods can achieve. One possibility is to weight the cable structure so that possible changes of load or wind loads remain low in comparison with the dead weight of the structure. This solution is available for suspended roofs, for example.

The disadvantage here is that the additional loads, usually applied in the form of prefabricated concrete parts, actually mean losing the advantages of the cable structure, and also that correspondingly large funicular forces have to be dissipated.

\\ Hint:
The cables in cable-stayed structures are made of high-strength steel. Many thin steel wires, with a diameter that varies according to cable type, are twisted around each other to form strands. These strands are then made into cables.

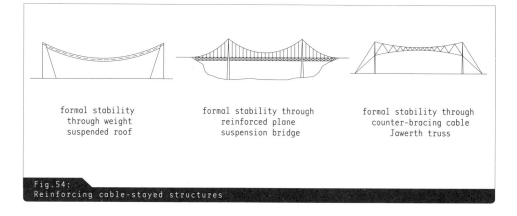

formal stability
through weight
suspended roof

formal stability through
reinforced plane
suspension bridge

formal stability through
counter-bracing cable
Jawerth truss

Fig.54:
Reinforcing cable-stayed structures

Another solution is reinforcement with flexurally rigid structural elements. In suspension bridges, for example, the suspended carriageway is so flexurally rigid that it reinforces the whole bridge.

A cable-stayed structure can also be reinforced by counterbracing with additional cables. This can be done in a variety of ways. Two-dimensional beams can be manufactured, e.g. the Jawerth truss, which is reminiscent of lattice structures, but actually has nothing in common with them. All the cables in systems of this kind are so highly pretensioned that no cable slackens, even under the highest possible load. This means that the structure remains stable in form and capable of loadbearing. › Fig. 54 In two-dimensional structural elements made up of cablenets, rigidity in the system is achieved by prestressing areas that curve in opposite directions to each other. › Chapter Plate structures

ARCH

If a loaded cable is fixed and turned over, we have a form that dissipates loads as compression forces, and not tensile forces. This is the ideal arch form, since, like a cable, it dissipates load only as normal forces.

Resistance line   This ideal form, which can be established by calculation or by a drawing method, is called a resistance line.

Arch and cable also have other things in common.

Arch height   The arch also dissipates vertical and horizontal forces in both supports, and as with the cable, the height of the arch, measured from floor or base level to apex, is linked with the magnitude of the horizontal forces: the shallower the arch, the greater the proportion of horizontal forces working as compression forces, known as arch thrust. › Fig. 56

Fig.55:
Arcuated loadbearing systems

The crucial difference between cable and arch lies in the fact that as solid arch, unlike a cable, cannot follow a change of load by changing its shape. A resistance line as an exact arch form applies only to an individual load position. If the load changes, the resistance line changes as well. This means that both normal force and bending moments are created in an arch. There are various ways in which arch structures can deal with these problems.

Masonry arches usually have a very large dead weight. Because the working load is small in comparison with the dead load, there are few consequences for the resistance line if it changes. The arch remains stable. Arches can also be reinforced with additional structural elements. For example, if masonry is raised round an arch in the form of a wall, it prevents the arch from deforming or losing its loadbearing capacity. It is also possible to make arches of rigid materials such as laminated timber or steel. Here, the static height of the arch support must be large enough to be able to absorb the moments as well as the normal forces. > Fig. 57

\\Tip:
Genuine arcuated loadbearing systems should not be confused with arcuated bending beams. An arch whose horizontal forces are not absorbed by both supports can dissipate its forces only by bending.

\\Hint:
Arcuated loadbearing systems are derived from masonry construction. Since masonry can absorb only compression forces, all the apertures have to be spanned by arches. Old masonry structures present an opportunity to study many sophisticated arcuated loadbearing systems and the skilful treatment of arch thrust.

Further information about masonry arches can be found in *Basics Masonry Construction* by Nils Kummer, Birkhäuser Verlag, Basel 2007.

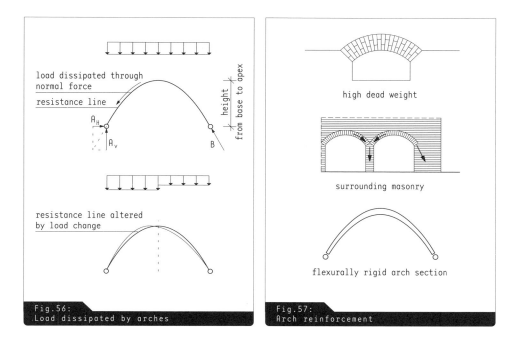

Fig.56:
Load dissipated by arches

high dead weight

surrounding masonry

flexurally rigid arch section

Fig.57:
Arch reinforcement

In arches, we distinguish between three different statical systems: two-articulated arches, three-articulated arches, and arches without articulation.

Two-articulated arch

A two-articulated arch has articulated supports. They absorb horizontal and vertical forces, but no moments. The question of what would happen if a support were lowered shows that this is a statically undetermined system.

Three-articulated arch

Adding one more articulation, usually at the apex of the arch, turns this statically undetermined into a statically determined system. This makes hardly any difference to the loadbearing properties, but the advantage in terms of construction engineering is that an arch is easier to transport in two parts. The articulation is created by the fact that the two parts of the arch are then simply leaned against each other at the apex and screwed together.

Arch without articulation (braced arch)

Bracing the supports makes the arch more rigid because the braces prevent any distortion caused by bending moments. The effect can be compared with columns supported as in Euler cases 2 or 4, and the bracing makes the structure more rigid here as well. Braced arches are statically undetermined. They are very rare because effective bracing requires a very elaborate construction. › Fig. 58

53

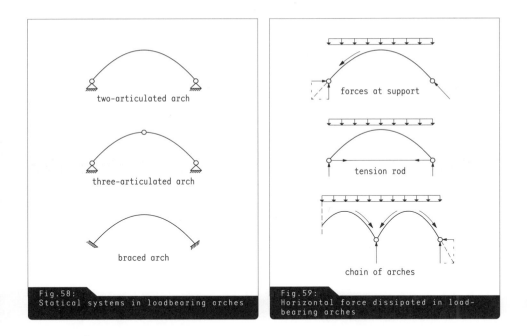

Fig.58:
Statical systems in loadbearing arches

Fig.59:
Horizontal force dissipated in loadbearing arches

There are various ways of handling the horizontal forces produced. Either the supports can be constructed so that they make it possible to dissipate the arch thrust, or a tension rod can be inserted between the supports to balance the horizontal forces in one with those in the other. If several arches are built adjacent to each other, the horizontal forces acting on the connected supports cancel each other out, so that only vertical forces have to be dissipated. > Fig. 59

FRAME

A simple loadbearing system consists of two columns with a beam or truss above them. But this system is not stable until the columns have articulated support at the top and bottom. Stability can be achieved by connecting the horizontal beam to the columns in a way that is flexurally rigid. This produces an efficient system, a frame.

In a frame, the horizontal members are called rails and the supports posts.

When the rails and posts are joined rigidly, they behave as though the beam is running "round the corner". So if the rail bends under a load, it also transfers the bending force into the posts. These would deflect outwards if they were not supported. The supports thus resist deformation and the

Arch thrust

Rail

Post

54

stresses are addressed by the structure as a whole. The posts also limit sagging in the rails. So each rail does not function like a simply supported beam, but is partially restrained.

This is also clear from the moment gradient. A characteristic feature of a frame is the moment at support created by the restraining effect of the posts in the corners of the frame. This reduces the moment of span of the frame rail. The advantage for the loadbearing capacity here is that of a continuous, as opposed to a simple, support. The moment at support reduces the moment of span, which means that the dimensions of the beam can be smaller. > Fig. 61

It also becomes clear that the corners of the frame are subject to a high load by the moment at support. They have to be constructed carefully, in order to have the required flexural strength. So that the simplest possible structural elements can be prefabricated, it makes sense to manufacture the rails and posts separately and join them together only at the building site. But this exacerbates the problem with the flexurally rigid corners, which nevertheless create another essential advantage for the system. We said at the outset that it is only the flexurally rigid corners that make the frame into a stable system. They reinforce it longitudinally, which is important for skeleton structures. A frame in a statical system has a similar function to a complete shear wall, and can be used to reinforce built structures. > Fig. 61 and Chapter Reinforcement

Two-articulated frame

The frames in Figure 59 are shown with two articulated supports. They are called two-articulated frames and, like two-articulated arches, are statically undetermined systems.

Three-articulated frame

A further articulation can be added to frames as well as to arches, to make the system statically determined. This makes very little difference to the loadbearing capacity, but the construction can benefit from it under certain circumstances, especially as this third articulation can be placed

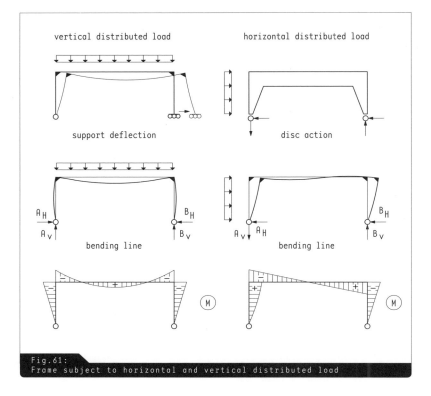

vertical distributed load

horizontal distributed load

support deflection

disc action

bending line

bending line

Fig.61:
Frame subject to horizontal and vertical distributed load

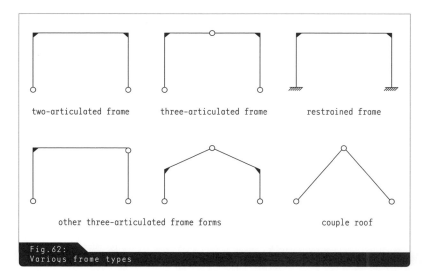

two-articulated frame

three-articulated frame

restrained frame

other three-articulated frame forms

couple roof

Fig.62:
Various frame types

in a variety of ways. It can be in the middle, in the ridge or even in a corner of the frame. Because the bending moments are zero at the articulation point, the construction can be more filigree here than in the areas with greater bending moments.

Restrained frame

The rigidity of frames can be further increased by bracing the posts into the supports. They are then called restrained frames, but are seldom used, because restraining the posts is a very elaborate process. > Fig. 62

LOADBEARING STRUCTURES

Buildings are complex three-dimensional structures, and at first their loadbearing systems seem immensely elaborate and difficult to analyse. But fundamentally all construction types are derived from two principles: solid construction and skeleton construction. These two principles have been applied since the earliest days of building, and all the techniques so far invented follow them; the same rules apply to ancient clay huts or pile dwellings as to the modern building industry's complex systems. Figure 63 shows a specimen ground plan as a solid structure, a skeleton structure and in some hybrid constructions.

SOLID CONSTRUCTION

Disc

Solid structures are made up of flat elements that dissipate vertical and horizontal loads. Wall-like discs can be loaded vertically as well as horizontally in their longitudinal direction. But conversely, they have barely any transverse loadbearing capacity, i.e. via their surface. › Fig. 64 Discs or walls can fail in a variety of ways; they can buckle or fall over. When building using solid techniques they are protected from this through reinforcement by other walls, placed at certain intervals adjacent to or intersecting them. The walls support each other mutually and this makes a sold structure stable.

Modular
construction
method

A structure of this type is also called modular. We distinguish between loadbearing, reinforcing and non-loadbearing walls. Non-loadbearing walls can be removed without affecting structural stability. Reinforcing walls are also deemed to be loadbearing in standards. As a rule, loadbearing walls are thicker, which enables them to dissipate the ceiling loads.

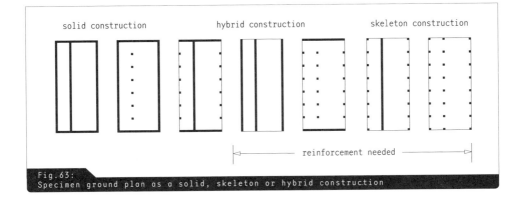

Fig.63:
Specimen ground plan as a solid, skeleton or hybrid construction

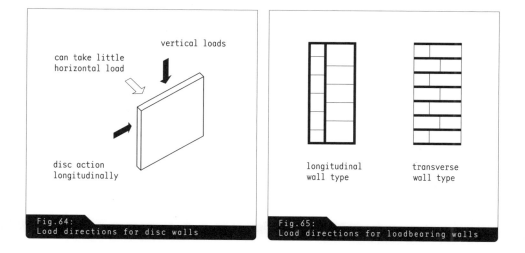

Fig.64:
Load directions for disc walls

Fig.65:
Load directions for loadbearing walls

Solid structures are divided into longitudinal and transverse wall types.

Longitudinal
wall type

If one or two loadbearing central walls run parallel to the long sides of the building, this is known as a longitudinal wall type; most simple, urban homes are built on this principle.

Transverse wall
type

The transverse wall type, also known as crosswall construction, is suitable for buildings such as hotels and terraced houses, where small rooms are the principal requirement. It is possible to make a distinction between these types when using floors with timber beams or prefabricated concrete parts with uniaxially directed stresses. When using concrete floors that dissipate their loads in several directions, longitudinal and transverse walls are usually loadbearing. › Fig. 65

\\Hint:
The terms solid or massive construction and skeleton construction do not mean the same thing for architects as they do for structural engineers. The above explanation is couched in architectural language, which is based on geometry and structure. For structural engineers, solid construction is a subject in its own right dealing with masonry and reinforced concrete. So structural engineers tend to link the term solid construction with the material.

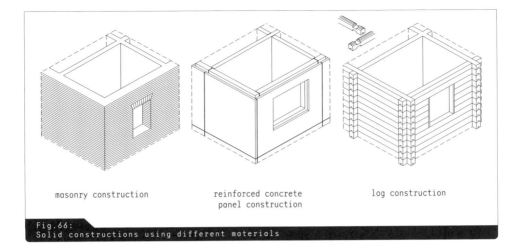

masonry construction   reinforced concrete   log construction
                         panel construction

Fig.66:
Solid constructions using different materials

Masonry

> 🔲

The original solid construction is the masonry building. Masonry walls cannot absorb tensile stresses, and have to be reinforced appropriately to their height, length and thickness. Tensile strains are best avoided by clear load dissipation without protrusions, shoring or wide apertures.

Concrete

The chapter on slabs explained that reinforced concrete can also absorb tension forces. This means that concrete walls are considerably more stable than masonry walls, and that solid structures in concrete can be designed with a much greater degree of freedom in relation to room sizes, spans, apertures and structural complexity. They can be cast in situ or constructed from prefabricated parts, which are made up either of small slabs or of wall elements the size of the room, known as large panels.

Panel construction method

Construction using large panels is the popular industrialized building method, and is usually known as large-panel or slab construction. The components are fixed together with steel structural elements and concrete to create a continuous, monolithic structure.

Timber

Although timber construction usually employs the skeleton methods, there are some structures that are better classified as solid construction.

Log construction method

The first is log construction, where timber sections are piled horizontally to construct walls. Walls of this kind are stabilized by the halving joints used for the timbers at the corners of rooms or the whole building. The timber industry has progressed in recent years to the extent that for a few years now there have been panel materials on the market that make panel construction possible. Some of these are panels glued together from planks, like laminated timber, and some are plywood panels

Fig.67:
Skeleton construction

made from boards layered crosswise. These panel materials make construction methods viable that are very different from traditional timber construction methods. These methods are still in development at the time of writing.

SKELETON CONSTRUCTION

Skeleton constructions are made up of bar-shaped elements forming a structure like scaffolding. Panel and wall elements are then added to this structure. The loadbearing structure and the elements that create the interior spaces are, in principle, two separate systems. › Fig. 68

Fundamentally, skeleton structures are made up of three kinds of structural elements: the columns, the floor beams including the floor structure, and the reinforcement structures that absorb horizontal forces. These structural elements are fitted appropriately to the material at nodal points, almost always with articulated joints. Joints are articulated if they are not rigid enough to act as a restraint. They do not have to take the form of a hinge or similar. In principle, any material that is both compression- and tension-resistant can be used for skeleton structures, for example, timber, steel or concrete. Each of these has its own construction methods, with a particular set of problems arising from the material and the methods used in jointing it.

Concrete   Probably the commonest material for skeleton structures is reinforced concrete, with both in-situ cast concrete and reinforced elements as viable possibilities. A solid reinforced concrete floor slab is normally used for in-situ concrete structures, and then only reinforcements and columns are needed. This simplicity also explains the flexibility and economic viability of the system. › Fig. 69a But floors, as point-supported flat structures, admit only limited spans. All the forces from the floor slabs have to be transferred into the columns, which means that the points of transition

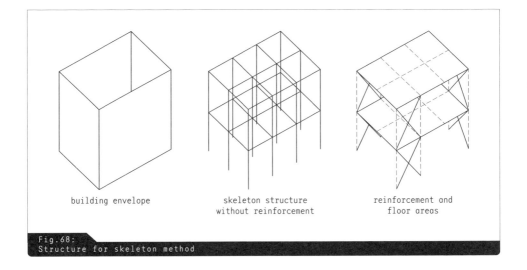

building envelope

skeleton structure
without reinforcement

reinforcement and
floor areas

Fig.68:
Structure for skeleton method

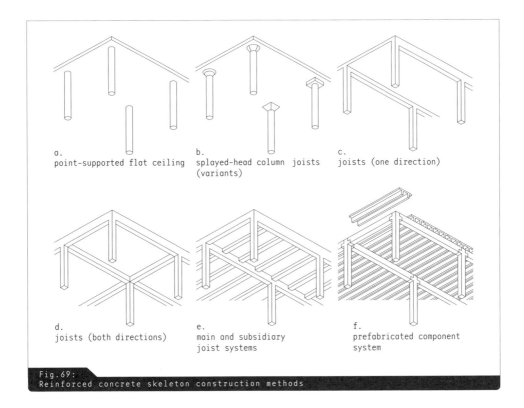

a.
point-supported flat ceiling

b.
splayed-head column joists
(variants)

c.
joists (one direction)

d.
joists (both directions)

e.
main and subsidiary
joist systems

f.
prefabricated component
system

Fig.69:
Reinforced concrete skeleton construction methods

from column to floor are very heavily loaded. There is a risk of the column punching through the floor slab.

Splayed-head columns
To avoid this, the edge can be reinforced in a different way. One method is to use "splayed-head columns". › Fig. 69b

Joists
If the spans are too great for this system, joists are used. These run from column to column like beams, and support the floor slabs on a linear pattern. Joists can be arranged in a number of different ways. According to the span, they are planned to run in one direction, in both directions, or as a system of main and subsidiary joists. › Fig. 69c, d, e

›◻
Skeleton structures can also be erected using prefabricated elements. There are various prefabricated systems containing components for ceilings, joists, columns and foundations. Transport to the building site is a crucial factor in terms of size. The structural elements should ideally not exceed the stipulated dimensions for a lorry-load in order to be financially viable. All that usually happens at the building site is that the parts are placed on top of one another and fixed securely into position. This means that the joints are articulated in principle.

Pi plates
Pi plates are often used as prefabricated floor components instead of flat floors. They are narrow plates with two ribs, and can be fitted together to make floor slabs. They work on the T-beam principle and thus make large spans possible. Floor slabs of this kind are laid on concrete beams that are supported on the column brackets in their turn. › Fig. 69f and Chapter Slab

Steel
Steel structures are almost always skeleton structures. They are usually built up of standard steel construction sections, called "rolled sections", in different profile series. › Fig. 70 The size needed is established by statical calculation.

Rolled sections
Rolled sections are produced to a height of up to 60 cm. If higher units are needed, they have to be welded from sheet metal; in steel construction, elements up to several centimetres thick are still known as sheets.

Corrugated sheets
Corrugated sheets are generally used if large areas have to be covered. They acquire their loadbearing capacity from their trapezoid folds,

◻

\\ Hint:
The nature of the floor structure greatly affects the clear height of each storey, so they should be included in the structural considerations as early as when the first sections are drawn. The greater the width of the floor spans, the greater their structural height.

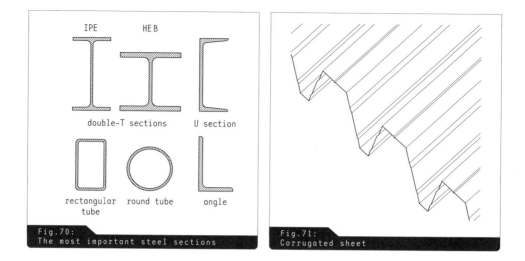

IPE   HE B

double-T sections   U section

rectangular   round tube   angle
tube

Fig.70:
The most important steel sections

Fig.71:
Corrugated sheet

and are able to function over large spans and serve as floor or roof structures. › Fig. 71

As a rule, steel structural elements are made in a steel construction workshop in transportable sizes and are then assembled on the building site. In the workshop, welding is the simplest and best method for manufacturing steel structural elements, but as welding is difficult on the building site, screws should be used for assembly connections.

It is possible to create flexurally rigid corners with an acceptable degree of effort and expense in steel construction. This means that columns and beams can be fitted together to form loadbearing frameworks to exploit their reinforcing capacities. › Chapter Frame To handle the very strong forces at the frame corners, the connections have to be much more powerful at these points. For example, for double-T sections, both flanges on a

\\Tip:
All the current construction reference works
give steel construction section tables with
precise dimensions and statical values. Generally speaking, sections from these series
should be used in construction, as they are
obtainable for any steel construction firm and
economical in use.

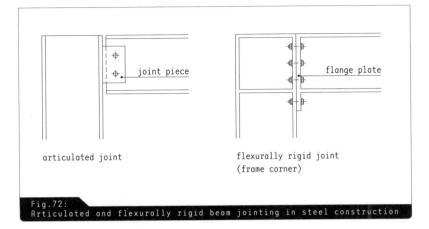

Fig. 72:

articulated joint

flexurally rigid joint
(frame corner)

joint piece

flange plate

Fig.72:
Articulated and flexurally rigid beam jointing in steel construction

horizontal member have to be fastened to the post with a flange plate, and the connecting screws should be as far away from each other as possible. Conversely, for an articulated joint, the rib can be screwed with a simple sheet metal joint piece. › Fig. 72

Fire protection

Although it seems remarkable at first, steel structures are at greater risk in fire than timber structures. Steel softens when heated to high temperatures, and quite quickly loses its entire loadbearing capacity. Steel must therefore always be protected from fire in high-rise buildings, for example by cladding loadbearing members with plaster or with a foaming paint.

Composite constructions

The rate at which the steel heats up in a fire can also be lowered by installing it in combination with concrete. For example, tubular steel profiles can be set in concrete in these composite constructions, or double-T sections filled with concrete. As well as slowing down the heating process, the concrete will ensure a certain residual loadbearing capacity in the event of fire. › Fig. 73

Timber

Timber is the earliest timber construction material. Various cultures have some very old, but very sophisticated timber construction techniques. This is a complex matter, because there are a number of construction methods and an infinite number of variants and mixtures between them. Here are the most important categories:

› 🛈
Traditional timber-frame construction

Traditional timber-frame construction is a pure form of skeleton construction filled with clay or brick. As a craft construction method, it is characterized by joints using skilfully created forms, without any metal connecting devices. Timber-frame buildings are seldom constructed like this any more, but they are often found in the field of heritage.

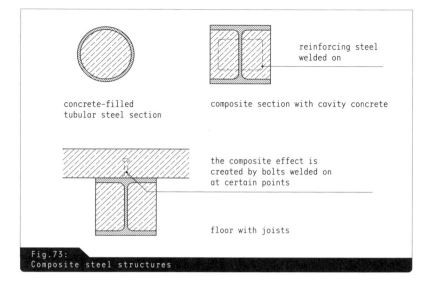

reinforcing steel
welded on

concrete-filled
tubular steel section

composite section with cavity concrete

the composite effect is
created by bolts welded on
at certain points

floor with joists

Fig.73:
Composite steel structures

Balloon and
platform frame
construction
American timber construction using the balloon and platform frame methods differs from traditional timber-frame construction in that it uses thin log- or plank-like timbers that would have no loadbearing capacity in their own right and would buckle if the timber cladding that forms the wall surface did not hold them in position. They work like ribs; they are stable with the cladding. The method is therefore sometimes called rib construction. Nailing is the principal jointing device. Constructions of this type are highly economical and flexible.

Engineering
timber skeleton
constructions
Modern engineering timber skeleton constructions have an ideal loadbearing system from a statical point of view, and can be constructed differently according to use. Materials such as laminated timber or various sheet products are used.

Modern timber-
frame
construction
Prefabrication is becoming increasingly accepted in timber skeleton construction. Here, wall and floor elements, in dimensions that can

\\ Hint:
More information on timber construction can be
found in *Basics Timber Construction* by Ludwig
Steiger, Birkhäuser Publishers, Basel 2007.

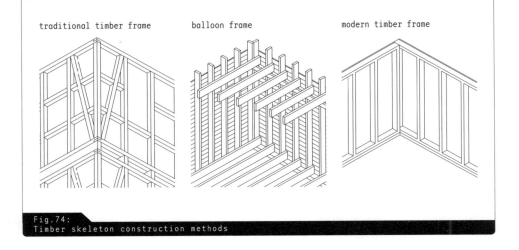

| traditional timber frame | balloon frame | modern timber frame |

Fig.74:
Timber skeleton construction methods

be transported on lorries, are preferred as component sizes. Timber-frame construction seems best suited to this. Prefabricated parts are manufactured consisting of derived timber sheets, onto which loadbearing sections are screwed. The parts can also be supplied with built-in insulation, cladding, windows or doors, and then fitted together. Similarly to the American methods, the frame sections work with the laminated wood areas to form a loadbearing framework. › Fig. 74

REINFORCEMENT

When planning skeleton constructions the key aim is usually to dissipate dead weight and vertical working loads, for which floors and columns are constructed. But attention must be paid to horizontal loads as well. The most important horizontal load is wind load, which can act on the building in any direction. Because the component joints are generally articulated, skeleton constructions have almost nothing to resist horizontal loads. They therefore need effective reinforcement, i.e. a construction that can transfer the horizontal loads from the façades into the foundations.

Reinforcing constructions function as a disc. They can accept horizontal forces longitudinally and dissipate them downwards. In tall buildings they work as vertical loadbearing members that can dissipate wind loads into the foundations from all floors.

Disc action

A disc can be solid, usually made of masonry or concrete. Disc action can also be created by a diagonal brace in one compartment of the skel-

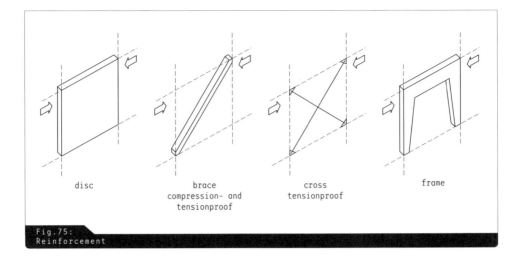

disc

brace
compression- and
tensionproof

cross
tensionproof

frame

Fig.75:
Reinforcement

eton structure. This brace reacts to compression for loads in one direction, and to tension for loads in the other. The same effect is achieved from two tensionproof crossing diagonals. › Fig. 75 The reinforcing action of frame systems was also pointed out in the chapter Frames.

Skeleton constructions have to be reinforced transversely and longitudinally. Reinforcement in each direction is not sufficient because, considering the ground plan, two disc elements always intersect at one point. This intersection would then be the point around which the loadbearing structure could twist and would collapse. To prevent this, we need a new plane of reinforcement, which can be positioned as wished, but it must not intersect with the other two at the same point. › Fig. 76a

Reinforcing structures can be arranged on the ground plan in different ways. But they should be placed near the centre, because otherwise the long section of the building would acquire a long lever arm around this reinforcement, thus creating powerful forces that would place an unnecessary strain on it.

Floor disc

If a skeleton construction is loaded horizontally, all the forces from one direction must be transferred into the wall disc provided for the purpose. This needs a rigid floor disc, as assumed in Figure 76. A floor can also consist of joists with a covering on top of them. A floor of this kind is not a disc, because the joists can shift in relation to each other. Not all the horizontal forces can be transferred into the reinforcing structure, but intermediate floors can easily be made into rigid discs by adding braces or cross-braces. › Fig. 77

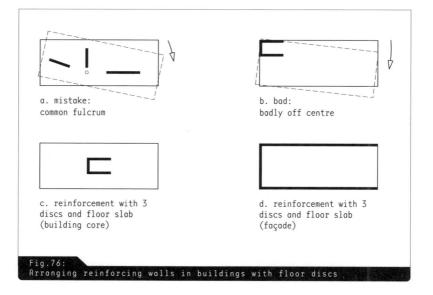

a. mistake:
common fulcrum

b. bad:
badly off centre

c. reinforcement with 3
discs and floor slab
(building core)

d. reinforcement with 3
discs and floor slab
(façade)

Fig.76:
Arranging reinforcing walls in buildings with floor discs

Building core

In high-rise buildings, building cores containing fire escapes and lift shafts are often used as reinforcing structures. They consist of mostly closed walls and run from the roof to the foundations, and can act as vertical loadbearing members. In high-rise building, it can be more problematic to dissipate the horizontal loads than the vertical ones, because wind speeds increase with the height of the building and the effect of the wind loads is much greater. Although the building core provides reinforcement in most high-rise buildings, one possibility is to make the whole façade of the building function into a vertical trussed girder, thus working with the maximum girder dimensions, i.e. the whole width of the building.

For architects, the key question is whether their design will be adequately reinforced or not, or put it another way, whether it is stable or not. In addition, a distinction is made between less rigid or more rigid loadbearing systems. This depends on how generously or how centrally the reinforcements are arranged. The different reinforcement methods do not have identical effects, and here too a distinction can be made between more or less rigid ones.

HALLS

The hall concept ultimately means little more than the fact that large spaces are enclosed, as they can be built using both solid and skeleton methods, and take any conceivable form. What they have in common is the

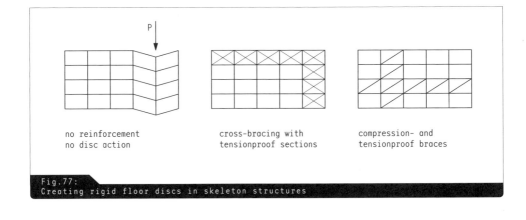

no reinforcement
no disc action

cross-bracing with
tensionproof sections

compression- and
tensionproof braces

Fig.77:
Creating rigid floor discs in skeleton structures

large span for the roof loadbearing structure. The roof geometry can also be designed in a variety of ways. It can be focused on draining the surface of the roof, on an advantageous shape for the roof girders, or on the way in which the skylights are built into the roof area.

Shed roof

Skylights can be placed longitudinally, or be constructed in the direction of the loadbearing structure and as an integral part of it, as in shed roofs. > Fig. 78

Halls thus need a roof loadbearing structure that can handle a large span. It is an advantage here to the make the roof area a lightweight structure, as the dead weight is an additional load on the structure as a whole.

A large number of statical systems are available for hall construction. The most common are described briefly below.

Truss

Long girders resting on columns or walls are also known as roof frames or trusses. Because their support points are articulated, a construction of this kind must be reinforced either by creating a rigid roof disc and the façades, or by bracing the columns. Roof trusses can be made of wood, steel or concrete. > Fig. 79

Arch

Arches make appropriate loadbearing structures for large spans, and thus for halls, because the loads are dissipated mainly as normal forces and not as bending forces. A solution must however be found for the great horizontal forces at support. The arches either run to the floor, so that the arch thrust can be transferred into the foundations directly, or they sit on columns or walls, which then have to be reinforced with structures such as buttresses. It is possible to use tie members between the supports to balance the horizontal forces on both sides. Then only the vertical forces have to be transferred into the walls. > Fig. 80 and Chapter Arch

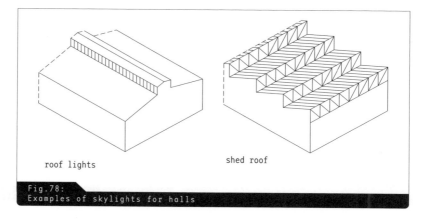

roof lights

shed roof

Fig.78:
Examples of skylights for halls

Frame

Frames are well suited to hall construction. They can be used to create all kinds of roof geometries, unlike arch constructions. Asymmetrical forms can also be implemented very well with two- and three-articulated frames. The section dimensions must however always match the moment gradient, which must be established for the particular geometry and load pattern. > Fig. 81 and Chapter Frame

Beam grid

The systems named so far consist of girders, spanning the space in one direction. These are directed systems. But it is also possible to design loadbearing structures that dissipate their loads on all sides. Load dissipation on several sides makes sense primarily for spaces with approximately equal spans in both directions. Here, the girders cross over each other, thus forming a grid. Girder grids of this kind can be made of various different materials. They can run through joists in conjunction with an in-situ cast concrete ceiling, and thus form a monolithic bond. Flexurally rigid connection of each intersection point is more laborious at the assembly stage for steel and timber.

Three-dimensional frameworks

Trussed girders can also be extended to form a three-dimensional loadbearing system. These are then called three-dimensional frameworks, and are defined by the design of the bar and node components. Three-dimensional frameworks are almost always made of prefabricated steel elements. > Fig. 82

Reinforcement

Reinforcement or stiffening for halls obeys the laws explained in the previous chapter. But other points must also be borne in mind. For example, reinforcing just one loadbearing axis is not sufficient for halls above a certain size, because the loads within the loadbearing structure travel a great distance before they are transferred, and so the structure as a whole would not be rigid enough.

72

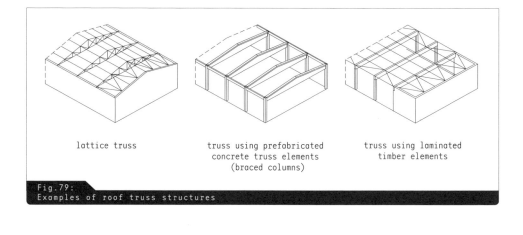

lattice truss

truss using prefabricated concrete truss elements (braced columns)

truss using laminated timber elements

Fig.79:
Examples of roof truss structures

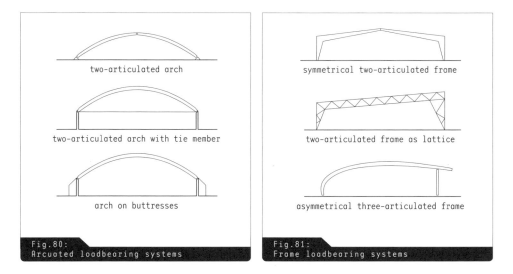

two-articulated arch

two-articulated arch with tie member

arch on buttresses

Fig.80:
Arcuated loadbearing systems

symmetrical two-articulated frame

two-articulated frame as lattice

asymmetrical three-articulated frame

Fig.81:
Frame loadbearing systems

Long girders dimensioned appropriately for their span are at risk of buckling in their transverse direction. › Fig. 44, p. 43 There is a risk of failure through great imposed loads, or through wind load against the gable. To prevent this, a joining construction is usually added at roof level to reinforce the gables and transfer the wind loads to the eaves. Adding members that run transversely to the girders, the purlins, means that the additional trusses are attached to the reinforced areas and thus prevented from buckling. › Fig. 83 and Chapter Reinforcement

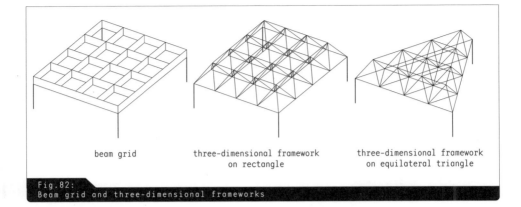

beam grid | three-dimensional framework on rectangle | three-dimensional framework on equilateral triangle

Fig. 82:
Beam grid and three-dimensional frameworks

Steel is an ideal material for hall construction. Steel loadbearing structures are light, have a high loadbearing capacity, and can be used to implement all conceivable statical systems economically. One great advantage here is that flexurally rigid joints can also be created easily.

Wood is also a very efficient material for hall construction. Arches, trusses or frames in laminated timber, or lattice trusses made of solid timber sections can be used. Flexurally rigid joints for frame systems can be created with laminated timber.

Concrete halls are always made from prefabricated parts. Their loadbearing systems differ from those in other halls in that the columns are usually clamped into the foundations, but the trusses are articulated at the support points. Reinforced concrete trusses are usually manufactured in adjustable steel formwork, so the system allows little flexibility in choosing the girder geometry.

PLATE STRUCTURES

The chapter Structural elements discussed arches and cables, which dissipate their loads as compression or tension forces, unlike girders subject to bending loads. This load dissipation principle can also be implemented in three dimensions by using plate structures. A large number of different concepts and many variants occur in their design. The most important groups are named below, to give a general idea.

Folded plates/ shells

Folded plates are made up of flat surfaces and acquire their loadbearing capacity from the disc action of these areas, while shells are curved loadbearing systems that can differ considerably in their forms. > Fig. 84

Beam-like plate structures

Shells or folded plates can span from support to support as long sections, like beams. Fitting them together then forms a roof. When handling

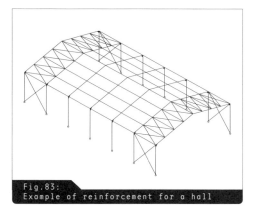

Fig.83:
Example of reinforcement for a hall

large spans, it is important to construct a great statical height with the lowest possible dead weight. Beam-like plate structures are very suitable for this, because of their curved or folded girder sections. Their loadbearing action is most closely allied to that of corrugated sheets. › Fig. 71, p. 65 Beam-like plate structures must be supported at the edges, to prevent them from collapsing as a result of lateral deflection. › Fig. 85

Tension-/com-
pression-loaded
plate structures

As with loadbearing systems based on arches and cables, plate structures are distinguished according to their loading type.

Domes and shells

Domes, shells and similar loadbearing structures are compression-loaded in some areas and tension-loaded in others. The more continuously their periphery can be supported, the better they will dissipate loads.

Cablenets
and membrane
constructions

Conversely, all suspended constructions, such as cablenets and membrane constructions, are only tension-loaded. Concrete structures can be tension-loaded as well. They are supported by flexurally rigid peripheral beams or cables. Peripheral cables of this kind then dissipate the powerful tensile forces through guys that run into foundations with tensionproof anchorage.

Single-/double-
curved surfaces

Single-curved surface curve in one direction, but are linear in the other. All curved surfaces that can be made from a flat surface, such as a sheet of paper, are single-curved. They are always sections of cylinders or cones. They can be supported at their ends, like beams, or on their long sides. Unlike beam support, a longitudinally supported, single-curve shell dissipates its loads according to form by the same action as an arch.

Double-curved means that the shells cannot be formed from flat surfaces. Figure 86 shows some examples of this. A double curve makes the surfaces rigid in three dimensions. It ensures that tension-loaded surfaces such as cablenets and membranes will not deform, provided there has been

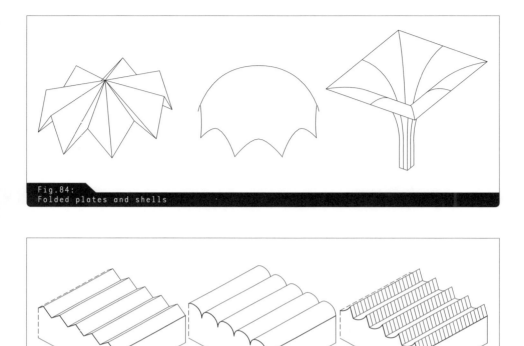

Fig.84:
Folded plates and shells

Fig.85:
Beam-like folded plates and shells

adequate pretensioning. Compression-loaded brick or concrete shells thus form loadbearing surfaces even when the material is not very thick.

Single- or coun-
ter-directional
curved surfaces Shells or domes are double-curved plate systems operating in one direction. Both curves point in the same direction. Counter-directional curved surfaces are also called saddle surfaces and usually occur in cable-nets or membrane constructions.

Shells or domes are double-curved plate systems operating in one direction. Both curves point in the same direction. Counter-directional curved surfaces are also called saddle surfaces and usually occur in cable-nets or membrane constructions.

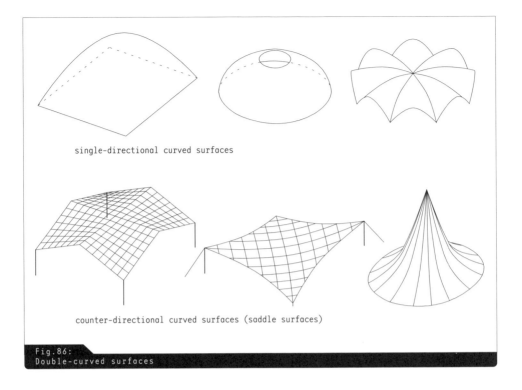

single-directional curved surfaces

counter-directional curved surfaces (saddle surfaces)

Fig.86:
Double-curved surfaces

FOUNDATIONS

Subsoil

The subsoil is part of the loadbearing structure, as well as the foundations, and like all the other structural elements it must be able to handle the forces it has to accept. Like every other building material, it responds to loads with deformations, which can involve sinking several centimetres. Sinking is thus a normal facet of loadbearing behaviour and is not deleterious.

The subsoil usually has a much lower loadbearing capacity than other building materials. In order to prevent the acceptable stresses being exceeded, the loads to which the building subjects it must be distributed over an adequately large foundation area. Loads spread over a wide area in the subsoil, which means that the stress under the foundation dissipates rapidly with increasing depth under the footing.

Soil type

There are many types of soil, and they respond to loads in different ways. The key factor affecting its properties is the grain size or the grain size mixture. The way the soil responds to fluctuations in humidity is also important. It is therefore essential to collect as much information

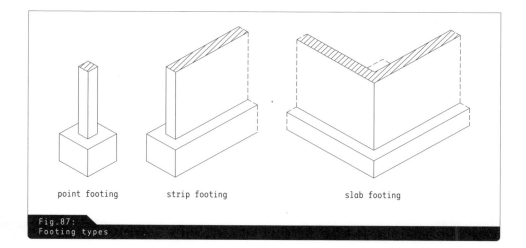

point footing   strip footing   slab footing

Fig.87:
Footing types

as possible about soil material and soil humidity, and about groundwater levels. A soil report is now a customary feature of smaller construction projects as well.

Footing types

Footings transfer loads into the subsoil. Soil stresses thus depend on the area across which the loads are distributed, i.e. on the size of the footing. A distinction is made between the following footing types:

_ Point footings are usually deployed to absorb the load from individual columns
_ Strip footings dissipate loads from walls, into the ground, for example
_ Slab footings consist of a continuous concrete base that distributes the loads from the walls and columns standing on over the whole area of the building. › Fig. 87

Footings can also be supplied to the building site in prefabricated form, although this makes financial sense mainly for point footings. Figure 88 shows a bucket footing, into which the column fits as if into a bucket. Once the prefabricated column has been adjusted precisely, the joint between the footing and the column is filled with mortar, thus bonding the two prefabricated elements securely.

Deep foundations

If no loadbearing subsoil is to be found in the upper strata, it is possible to dissipate the loads by using deep foundations. To do this, holes are drilled down to the firm stratum and then filled with concrete. These bored piles then act as long columns on which the building stands in the

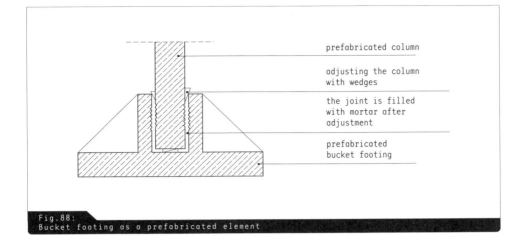

prefabricated column

adjusting the column with wedges

the joint is filled with mortar after adjustment

prefabricated bucket footing

Fig.88:
Bucket footing as a prefabricated element

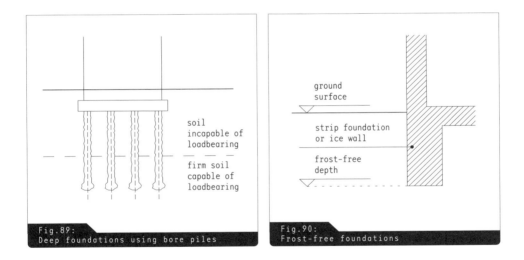

soil incapable of loadbearing

firm soil capable of loadbearing

Fig.89:
Deep foundations using bore piles

ground surface

strip foundation or ice wall

frost-free depth

Fig.90:
Frost-free foundations

subsoil. The loads are then largely transferred via the tip of the bored pile, but a firm hold in the subsoil can also be gained via the roughly concreted surface shell of the pile. › Fig. 89

Frost-free foundations

When the ground freezes, it expands because of the increased volume of the ice it contains. This produces perceptible uneven soil deformations. It is therefore necessary to avoid frost action under the footings. The ground only freezes to a certain depth below the surface in winter,

so a continuous strip foundation is laid around the edge of the building, extending into the frost-free area underground. The required depth depends on the climate and can be anything from 80 cm to over a metre.
> Fig. 90

Damaged
foundations

Cracks in the completed building usually indicate damaged foundations. Such damage is always the result of irregularities, possibly in the building, possibly in the subsoil.

Changing soil properties inevitably cause problems, because generally speaking each soil type is subject to different degrees of sinking. In terms of the building, problems can arise because parts of the building that impose very different loads share foundations, or from having foundations at different depths, because this will always cause different tensions in the subsoil. It this is recognized at the planning stage, suitable measures can be taken, either to dissipate the loads into the soil evenly, or to avoid possible damage from different sinking rates, for example by means of gaps in the structure.

IN CONCLUSION

Basics Loadbearing Systems is intended to provide an approach to the complex field of loadbearing system theory. The knowledge collected here should enable students to understand structural contexts, to consider the demands made by support and loads when designing, and thus to plan their designs realistically and holistically. Designing the loadbearing structure ultimately helps to sharpen designers' ideas of space and can also further them by working creatively with the possibilities that supporting structures offer. Thus, the quality of the loadbearing structure design is assessed first and foremost by whether it flows from the design idea, or even helps to shape it. This happens primarily in the planning tasks whose function and structure make the loadbearing system the determining element – such as when using large spans. Problems of this kind can usually be solved only by addressing the design of the loadbearing system in its full complexity.

Thus, the basics this volume conveys can be expanded upon as part of the student's own architectural development process by working creatively or even playfully with loadbearing structures, and by interpreting the laws of support structures in terms of individual requirements. To sum up, there are three basic principles to be considered:

1. Loadbearing structural elements should run through all floors to the foundations in a single line.
2. Spans should be kept as small as possible. Large spans demand a great deal of expense and effort. They should be deployed only when large spaces expressly demand them.
3. It is possible to handle large spans without difficulty if sufficient height is allowed to construct them. Even if nothing is known at this stage about the nature of the structure, sufficient statical height should simply be allowed for such spans.

Anyone who would like to go beyond the material introduced in this book and find out more about loadbearing structures will gain a better understanding of how structural engineers work; it is then possible for students to make their own calculations, thus increasing their ability to determine dimensions more precisely, and enabling themselves to design on the basis of the loadbearing structure itself.

APPENDIX

PRE-DIMENSIONING FORMULAE
The formulae below can provide provisional results for dimensioning structural components at the preliminary design stage. They do not furnish conclusive proof of loadbearing capacity.

Floors and ceilings
Concrete floors or ceiling as flat units in multi-storey buildings:
_ Viable at spans up to 6.5 m
_ The formulae apply to simply supported beams
_ Thickness to provide necessary sound insulation at least 16 cm
_ As a point-supported flat ceiling or carried on walls

at a span less than 4.3 m

$$h(m) \approx \frac{l_i(m)}{35} + 0.03 \text{ m}$$

at a span greater than 4.30 m and given limited deflection as a result of light dividing walls on the floor

$$h(m) \approx \frac{l_i{}^2(m)}{150} + 0.03 \text{ m}$$

Timber beam floor or ceiling:
_ Distance between beams 70–90 cm
_ Width of beams $\approx 0.6 \cdot d \geq 10$ cm

Height of beams $\quad h \approx \dfrac{l_i}{17}$

IPE girders:
_ Load around the strong axis
_ Where h = section height in cm, q = distributed load in KN/m, l = span in m

$$h \approx \sqrt[3]{50 \cdot q \cdot l^2} - 2$$

HEB girders:
_ Load around the strong axis
_ Where h = section height in cm, q = distributed load in KN/m, l = span in m

$$h \approx \sqrt[3]{17.5 \cdot q \cdot l^2} - 2$$

Wide-span roof-bearing structures

Laminated timber beams (parallel):
_ Span 10–35 m
_ Distance between trusses 5–7.5 m

Height $\quad h = \dfrac{l}{17}$

Timber trussed beams with parallel chords:
_ Span 7.5–60 m
_ Distance between trusses 4–10 m

Overall height $\quad h \geq \dfrac{l}{12}$ to $\dfrac{l}{15}$

Steel solid web girder:
_ Span up to 20 m
_ IPE girder up to 600 mm high

Girder height $\quad h \approx \dfrac{l}{30} \cdots \dfrac{l}{20}$

Steel trussed girder:
_ Span up to 75 m

Girder height $\quad h \approx \dfrac{l}{15} \cdots \dfrac{l}{10}$

LITERATURE

James Ambrose: *Building Structures*, 2nd edition, John Wiley & Sons 1993

James Ambrose, Patrick Tripeny: *Simplified Engineering for Architects and Builders*, John Wiley & Sons 1993

Francis D.K. Ching: *Building Construction illustrated*, 3rd edition, John Wiley & Sons 2004

Andrea Deplazes (ed.): *Constructing Architecture*, Birkhäuser, Basel 2005

Heino Engel: *Structure Systems*, Hatje Cantz, Stuttgart 1997

Thomas Herzog, Michael Volz, Julius Natterer, Wolfgang Winter, Roland Schweizer: *Timber Construction Manual*, Birkhäuser, Basel 2003

Russell C. Hibbeler: *Structural Analysis*, 6th edition, Prentice Hall Publisher 2005

Friedbert Kind-Barkauskas, Bruno Kauhsen, Stefan Polonyi, Jörg Brandt: *Concrete Construction Manual*, Birkhäuser, Basel 2002

Angus J. Macdonald: *Structure and Architecture*, 2nd edition, Architectural Press 2001

Bjørn Normann Sandaker, *The Structural Basis of Architecture*, Whitney Library of Design, New York 1992

G.G. Schierle: *Structure in Architecture*, USC Custom Publishing, Los Angeles 2006

Helmut C. Schulitz, Werner Sobek, Karl-J. Habermann: *Steel Construction Manual*, Birkhäuser, Basel 2000

PICTURE CREDITS

Figure page 8:	Colonnade in front of the Old National Gallery, Berlin, Friedrich August Stüler
Figure page 34:	AEG Turbine Hall, Peter Behrens
Figure page 58:	Berlin Central Station, von Gerkan, Marg und Partner
Figure 7, left, right;	Institut für Tragwerksplanung,
Figure 41, left, centre;	Professor Berthold Burkhardt, Technische
Figure 55, left, right:	Universität Braunschweig

All other figures are supplied by the author.

Series editor: Bert Bielefeld
Conception: Bert Bielefeld, Annette Gref
Layout and Cover design: Muriel Comby

Translation from German into English:
Michael Robinson
English Copy editing: Monica Buckland

Library of Congress Control Number: 2007923624

Bibliographic information published by
the Deutsche Nationalbibliothek.
The Deutsche Nationalbibliothek lists this
publication in the Deutsche Nationalbibliografie;
detailed bibliographic data are available on the
Internet at http://dnb.ddb.de.

This book is also available in a German
(ISBN 978-3-7643-8091-5) and a French
(ISBN 978-3-7643-8106-6) language edition.

© 2007 Birkhäuser Verlag AG
Basel · Boston · Berlin
P.O. Box 133, CH-4010 Basel, Switzerland
Part of Springer Science+Business Media

Printed on acid-free paper produced from
chlorine-free pulp. TCF ∞
Printed in Germany

ISBN 978-3-7643-8107-3
9 8 7 6 5 4 3 2 1   www.birkhauser.ch